DIY CANNING

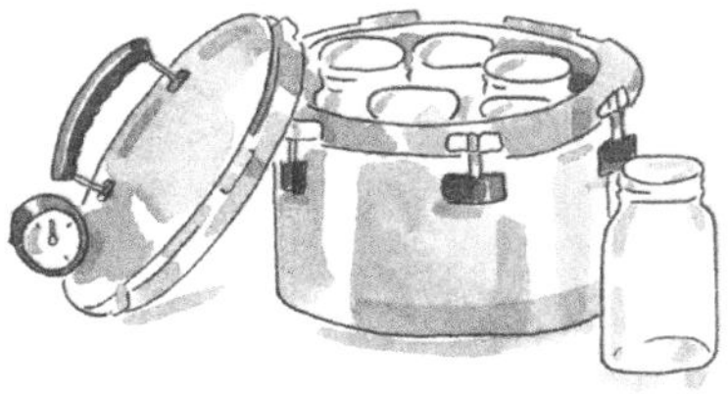

YOU CAN DO IT!

Capture the flavors of the season and enjoy them all year round with these simple, small-batch canning recipes.

Start by organizing your kitchen with the right equipment and canning ingredients.
(See page 16)

Select produce that is fresh and ripe; seasonal ingredients are usually a wise choice.
(See page 26)

If you're new to water-bath canning, a classic strawberry jam recipe is a great place to start.
(See page 30)

For those eager to try pressure canning, you can't go wrong with a simple recipe for green beans.
(See page 33)

DIY CANNING

OVER 100 SMALL-BATCH RECIPES FOR ALL SEASONS

ROCKRIDGE
PRESS

Rockridge Press, 2015

For general information on our other products and services or to obtain technical support, please contact our Customer Care Department within the U.S. at (866) 744-2665, or outside the U.S. at (510) 253-0500.

Rockridge Press publishes its books in a variety of electronic and print formats. Some content that appears in print may not be available in electronic books, and vice versa.

Cover photography © Stockfood/Don Crossland (front cover) and Stockfood/Katharine Pollak (back cover); Interior photography © Stockfood/Evi Abeler, p. 2 & 9; Stocksy/Canan Czemmel, p. 2 & 27; Stockfood/Katharine Pollak, p. 3; Stocksy/Gillian van Niekerk, p. 6; Stockfood/Valérie Lhomme, p. 10; Shutterstock/Kati Molin, p. 27; Stocksy/Sara Remington, p. 27; Stocksy/Raymond Forbes LLC, p. 27; Stockfood/Uwe Merkel, p. 28; Stockfood/Richard Jung Photography, p. 41; Stockfood/Wissing, Michael, p. 42; Stockfood/Sandra Krimshandl-Tauscher, p. 78; Stockfood/Scott Glen, p. 98; Stockfood/Kai Schwabe, p. 132; Stocksy/Laura Stolfi, p. 150; Stockfood/ Tony Hurley, p. 182; Stockfood/Gräfe & Unzer Verlag/Coco Lang, p. 204; Stockfood/Don Crossland, p. 252

ISBN: Print 978-1-62315-439-4 | eBook 978-1-62315-440-0

CONTENTS

INTRODUCTION

If you close your eyes and imagine, can you taste those summer tomatoes still warm from the vine? Hear the snap of the green beans freshly picked? Smell the strawberries even before you've reached the pick-your-own fields? Do you crave your favorite fresh seasonal produce year-round? Well, you can have it!

Stop craving and start canning! With the simple process of home canning, you can put up a bounty of fresh fruits, vegetables—and even meats—to enjoy whenever you please, in any season you please. Ditch the routine of buying salty canned goods from the grocery store, and take a step toward self-sustaining by joining the world of canning. Once you start, you will never look back!

If you're a beginner, no worries. The introductory chapters will get you well acquainted with the "dos and don'ts," basic terminology, and the process of canning as a whole. You'll be armed with the facts and be relieved of any concerns about this relatively simple practice.

Ditch the routine of buying salty canned goods from the grocery store, and take a step toward self-sustaining by joining the world of canning. Once you start, you will never look back!

When you're ready to begin, try your hand with one of the practice recipes. The comprehensive instructions will guide you to success and ensure all your questions are addressed. From there, you can begin to explore other recipes and discover an enjoyable way to spend a day or two preparing foods you can savor later—a small amount of time for the abundance of delicious, healthy foods to enjoy and share for months to come.

If you're an experienced canner, jump right in. If you need a refresher or haven't canned in some time, chapter one and chapter two offer new information and will bring you up-to-date with current recommendations and new safety guidelines. Things change, and being knowledgeable of today's best practices ensures that you'll create safe and pantry-stable foods to enjoy at a later date.

DIY Canning provides all the information you need to know to begin, including 80 water bath–canning and 24 pressure-canning recipes. It offers a variety of seasonal recipes for those delectable ingredients that come and go too quickly each year. You'll also find classic recipes to put up standards like tomatoes, berries, and apples. Advice and anecdotes from canning professionals will put you at ease. The ample canning tips throughout will help improve your process, offer new ideas, and guide you on the path to canning success—and a bountiful pantry.

Once you complete a project, assess the quality of your finished product with the evaluation worksheet. As you track your successes and failures you'll become a more accomplished food preserver.

It will happen—there will invariably be some jams or jellies that do not set, some jars that break, or some foods that discolor. By learning from your mistakes, you can achieve greater success; create delicious, safely canned foods from your own kitchen; and entice others to join you on this delicious journey.

Happy canning!

I FUNDAMENTALS

1

HOME CANNING BASICS

A BRIEF HISTORY OF CANNING

Canning, by definition, is the process of preserving food by packing it into cans or jars and heating to the appropriate temperature for the appropriate amount of time to inactivate enzymes and destroy microorganisms. During this process, a vacuum seal is formed, which prevents the recontamination of food during storage. While the process has changed and evolved significantly since its origins, this definition continues to be accurate today.

As food preservation methods go, canning is relatively new. Fermenting and drying methods have been around since before recorded history, but canning only made its first appearance toward the end of the eighteenth century. It developed out of a need to keep food safe and fresh for troops in combat: Napoleon Bonaparte offered a cash prize to anyone who could create a means to do so. After 15 years of experimentation, Nicholas Appert was the first to answer the call when he realized that a combination of heat and a proper seal were the necessary components to canned food preservation.

Let's fast-forward nearly three-quarters of a century to the year 1858, notable for the introduction of the seemingly ubiquitous Mason jar. By this time, commercial canning operations were in full swing in Europe, but this was the first time preserving foods by jar was accessible to the home cook. Over the following decades, William Charles Ball and Alexander Kerr, each working independently of the other for their own companies, invented many of the products still used today. Examples include the familiar wide-mouth canning jar and two-piece canning lid with a built-in seal.

TWO CANNING PROCESSES

There are two distinct types of canning, each requiring different supplies and used for different food types:

- **Water-bath canning** is a method that involves submerging filled jars in a canner, or pot, filled with boiling water. It is used for *high-acid foods* such as jams, jellies, salsas, and chutneys.
- **Pressure canning** is a process where pressure enables the temperature in the canner to rise above what it naturally would in an open environment. It is used for *low-acid foods.* Foods that are pressure canned include some vegetables, soups, stews, and meats.

WATER-BATH CANNING

Water-bath canning is used specifically for ***high-acid*** foods, those with a ***pH of 4.6 or lower***. This includes most (but not all) types of fruits, as well as foods that have been acidified to allow for this type of processing, such as tomatoes, pickles, and relishes. Acidifying is done by adding lemon juice, lime juice, vinegar, or citric acid to foods during preparation. They then have a pH low enough to be considered a high-acid food.

Of the two processes, water-bath canning is the simplest as it requires very little specialized equipment. Food is prepared according to specific recipes to keep the acid level accurate, and then packed into jars. Based on the type of food being canned, the jars are filled to different levels leaving a predetermined amount of headspace, which allows an adequate seal to form.

As a general rule, headspace requirements are:

- ¼ inch for jams, jellies, preserves, and spreads
- ½ inch for all other high-acid foods: tomatoes, fruits, pickles
- 1 inch for low-acid food

Exceptions include food items that need to be submerged, such as tomatoes or pickles. In these cases, depending on the cut of the vegetable, the instructions may suggest you pack less in the jar and then completely cover it with the brine.

The lids and rings are then fixed onto the jars. The sealed jars are placed into the canner, or large pot, already filled about halfway with hot water. Once the jars are in place, more hot water can be added to the canner, if needed. *The water must cover the jars by one to two inches.* The lid is placed on the canner, and the water is brought to a rolling boil (212°F, as measured by a candy thermometer). Once the water boils, the timer is started, signifying the beginning of the processing time. Depending on the product, the processing time can range from 5 to 90 minutes. To ensure proper canning safety, the water *must continue to boil steadily during this time.*

Any large pot can serve as a water-bath canner. However, there are plenty of specialized water-bath canning pots designed to hold quart jars, which can be a bit too large for a stockpot when elevated on a rack. A rack supports the jars away from the bottom of the pot to prevent direct contact with the burner and minimize breakage. It also allows for constant and even heat exchange.

The boiling process works by removing oxygen from the jars and helping form a seal. This seal protects the jars from contamination after processing. The heat readily kills the yeast, mold, and bacteria inherently present in the food. This process, though, is not sufficient to kill *Clostridium botulinum* spores, which cause the toxin botulism. But since these foods have a pH of 4.6 or lower, the spores are unable to grow in the high-acid environment, rendering the food safe for storage and consumption.

> The processing times listed for each recipe in *DIY Canning* are appropriate for anyone canning at sea level up to 1,000 feet in altitude. If you live at a higher elevation, you'll need to adjust the processing times to account for this. Refer to Appendix A: Altitude Adjustments (see page 233) to determine the correct processing time for your altitude.

Home canners generally consider water-bath canning the "safer" of the two canning types because it carries little risk. Both types of canning, though, are really rather simple. The biggest advantage of water-bath canning is that it requires little investment compared to pressure canning. Once you buy the jars and lids, a couple of inexpensive tools, and a large pot to use as your canner, you are ready to begin.

PRESSURE CANNING

For safety reasons, pressure canning is used for *all low-acid foods*, those with a *pH higher than 4.6*. This includes all types of meat, fish, poultry, and seafood, as well as most fresh vegetables. The high pH level in these foods means their low acid level allows the *Clostridium botulinum* spores to grow. The canning process for these products must then kill not only molds, yeasts, and bacteria, but also these toxic spores.

Clostridium botulinum spores can produce a deadly toxin (botulism) when left unchecked in an anaerobic (no oxygen) environment, such as in jars of canned food. These spores can be killed only by using a pressure canner for processing. A pressure canner uses pressure to raise the temperature inside the jars to 240°F, the temperature that can effectively kill these hazardous spores, rendering the food safe for storage and later consumption.

While you can use a stockpot for water-bath canning, a specialized pressure canner is required when canning all low-acid foods. Don't confuse this with a pressure cooker, which is a different type of cooking device. Buying a pressure canner is a considerable investment but, when well maintained, one that will produce an abundantly stocked pantry for many years.

There are two types of pressure canners: those with a gasket and those without a gasket. The kind with a gasket is typically less expensive, but the gasket needs to be replaced every year or so. Both types use locks or screws to hold the lid in place throughout the cooking time.

FROM THE MASTERS

JESSICA QUON AND SABRINA VALLE, CO-FOUNDERS OF THE JAM STAND
http://thej.am

The best thing about canning food is that you are creating something delicious instead of letting it go to waste. We encourage people to start with basic recipes and build on them, never skipping any steps. If you are completely new to canning, start with a small test batch and take it one step at a time so you don't overwhelm yourself. Always make sure that you can your jams at high heat, and use lids that pop to be extra safe. To reduce the chances of burning or overcooking your preserves, have everything prepped before you begin cooking anything.

When we first started, we had no idea of what we were doing. Our first canning experience was a nightmare, mainly because we did not do enough research and bought ingredients before we'd even looked up a recipe or reviewed the processing instructions. We purchased grapes as the base fruit for our first jam, a decision we later regretted because the recipe's instructions had us peeling the skin off each individual grape! After thirty minutes of peeling what felt like an endless number of grapes, we gave up and headed back to the store, where we purchased some peaches. Peaches are much easier to work with, and that night, we successfully peeled, cooked, and canned our first batch of peach jam. In case you're wondering, that experience was the inspiration for our tagline "...because there's so much more than grape jelly."

When we started The Jam Stand, all we had was passion and a desire to be creative in the kitchen. We signed up for a few farmers' markets and asked a lot of people in the industry for advice. Everyone was extremely helpful and supportive, and today, we've managed to grow our business into an artisanal jam company that's a true reflection of ourselves. Having a best friend and partner by your side as you get through a 12-hour jam session makes a huge difference; together, we think "outside of the jar" to create fun, funky flavors like our seasonal Chai Heart Pumpkin Jam and our signature Drunken Monkey Jam (made with sugar-coated bananas, rum, and lime). The process involves a lot of test batches and playing around with different flavor profiles, but it's all worth it because the results can be JAMAZING!

The other distinction between pressure canners is whether they are fitted with a weighted gauge or a dial gauge to track the canner's pressure. Measured in pounds per square inch (psi), *maintaining an even pressure is one of the most important steps in pressure canning.* Both dial gauges and weighted gauges are easy to use. The weighted gauge requires a little less monitoring during processing as its distinctive rattle can be heard while you're working on other projects close by. The dial gauge requires you to visibly monitor it throughout the processing time.

Based on your location, it is important to adjust for altitude when pressure canning. Unlike water-bath canning where longer processing times are used for higher elevations, *the adjustment in pressure canning relates to the amount of pressure used.* All pressure requirements and processing times in *DIY Canning* recipes are for people living at sea level up to 1,000 feet in altitude. If you live at a higher elevation, refer to Appendix A: Altitude Adjustments (see page 233) for the appropriate pressure needed or correct processing time for your altitude.

When you are ready to begin pressure canning, do not fear. This process is as simple as water-bath canning but gets a bad rap due to the potential risks. If you follow trusted recipes and processing times, there is no need to worry about the safety of your food.

LOW-ACID CANNING VERSUS HIGH-ACID CANNING

The difference between water-bath canning (*high-acid*) and pressure canning (*low-acid*) comes down to one very serious factor—botulism. *Clostridium botulinum*, the deadly toxin that causes botulism, requires two main factors to grow. First, it needs an *anaerobic* (no oxygen) environment, easily satisfied by the conditions inside a sealed jar where the oxygen has been removed. And, second, a *low-acid environment*, meaning it can only grow in foods with a pH above 4.6.

High-acid foods, such as fruits, jam, pickles, and relishes, still contain these spores after processing but they are unable to activate in the high-acid environment, effectively keeping the foods safe.

Low-acid foods, such as meats, vegetables, and soups, however, are still able to grow these spores even when sealed in a jar. For this reason, low-acid foods must be processed in a pressure canner. The pressure canner uses pressure (hence, its name) to bring the temperature of the jars' contents above that of boiling water (212°F) to 240°F— a temperature that kills the spores and makes the food safe for storage and future consumption.

The amount of low-acid foods that can be safely canned far outweighs the ones that can't. However, there are some foods that ***cannot*** be safely canned, even in a pressure canner. These include:

- Dairy products, foods containing dairy products, and imitation dairy products, including buttermilk, cheese, coconut milk, cream, milk, and soy milk
- Dried beans that have not been rehydrated and partially cooked
- Eggs
- Fats such as butter, lard, mayonnaise, and oils (with the exception of a small amount in a recipe)
- Foods that have been thickened with arrowroot, corn starch, flour, or any other thickener
- Grains, including barley, corn, rice, and wheat
- Mashed meats and vegetables (mashed potatoes, pumpkin, etc.)
- Pasta

IN THE KITCHEN

In your enthusiasm to get started, you can break the bank buying a ton of canning equipment and supplies, but you really need very little to begin, especially when water-bath canning. Start with the necessities and, as you go, decide whether you really need more supplies or can repurpose some other kitchen items to suit your needs.

ESSENTIAL EQUIPMENT

Some items are essential. The list is short, but these are the absolute basics to get you started.

PRESERVING POT. You need a sturdy non-reactive pot to cook most items in these recipes before canning them. A 6- to 10-quart stockpot is fine and gives you plenty of room to quickly cook down jams or simmer broths. Wider is better, as the increased surface area allows for quicker cooking. Stainless steel or enameled cast iron are two recommended choices. The only rule is do not use a reactive metal such as plain cast iron or aluminum. These can leave a strong taste in acidic foods.

WATER-BATH CANNER. For water-bath canning, you will need an additional large pot. This can be the large enameled variety that comes with its own rack and is specifically designed for canning, or you can fashion your own. While specialty canning pots are functional and allow you to can quarts easily, they can be cumbersome in a small kitchen and can quickly become

covered in rust. If you do use a specialty canning pot, dry it thoroughly between uses to extend its life.

Otherwise, simply use a **large stockpot**, especially for most of the small-batch recipes. The one thing you will need, however, is some sort of canning rack or other improvised tool that serves the same function. A small metal cake rack works well, as do several jar rings tied together with twist ties. In a pinch, a towel can also work. You can find several kinds of small rust-free canning racks online and in specialty stores that make canning in any large pot extremely easy. The reason for the rack is to keep the jars from directly contacting the bottom of the pot where the heat is strongest, as this can cause breakage.

PRESSURE CANNER. For canning low-acid foods, a pressure canner is essential. As noted previously, don't confuse this with a pressure cooker. These are two different devices. The investment in a pressure canner is considerable but, when properly cared for, it will serve you well for many years of canning. There are two types of pressure canners: those that close with a gasket (Presto) and those that do not (All American). Pressure canners with a gasket are generally less expensive but require a yearly gasket replacement, costing about $10.

Another consideration when selecting a pressure canner is what kind of **gauge** you prefer to monitor the pressure. The options are *weighted gauges* and *dial gauges*.

- Dial gauges require more vigilance to ensure that constant pressure is maintained throughout the canning process. The distinctive rattle of weighted gauges is audible and, therefore, requires less monitoring. Dial gauges must be tested annually to ensure they function properly for safe use.
- Weighted gauges do not need annual testing. If you opt for a weighted gauge pressure canner, buy a three-piece gauge so you can adjust between 5, 10, or 15 psi. The standard one-piece weighted gauge achieves 15 psi only.

JARS. Stock up on jars before you begin canning, inspecting any old jars for chips or cracks, especially on the rims. Review the recipes and determine which sizes you need. Using a wide-mouth versus a regular-mouth jar is your choice, but use the correct jar size listed in the recipe for accurate processing times. Most of the recipes use half-pint and pint jars, though some use quarter-pint and quart jars. Double check before you start a project.

Old glass jars from items such as peanut butter or mayonnaise are *not* suitable for canning. These are manufactured as single-use jars and not

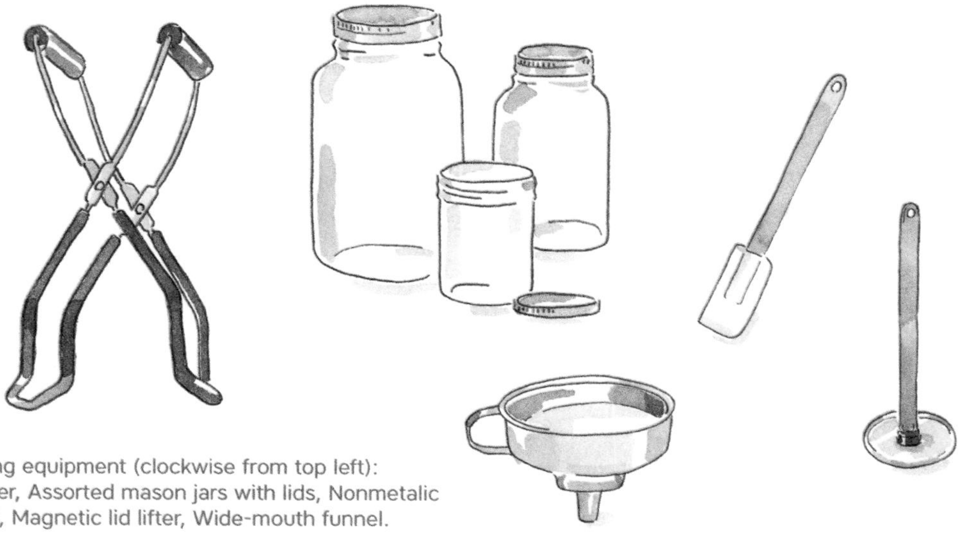

Canning equipment (clockwise from top left): Jar lifter, Assorted mason jars with lids, Nonmetalic utensil, Magnetic lid lifter, Wide-mouth funnel.

designed for repeated use. You'll likely have people telling you otherwise, but you take the chance of breakage and food loss when you use these.

When reusing old jars for a project, always remember to inspect the jars to ensure they are free of chips or cracks, paying special attention to the rims.

LIDS AND RINGS. Two-piece lids are the most common type and are widely available in both Kerr and Ball brands. The lids are designed for single use only, so keep extras on hand for each new project. They are inexpensive and easily purchased at many grocery stores, hardware stores, specialty retailers, and online. If you have an older box of lids purchased before 2014, they need to be heated to soften the sealing compound. To do so, place them in a saucepot filled with water and lightly simmer until they are needed. Do not boil them, as this can negatively affect the sealing compound.

You can also get reusable Tattler lids that work in much the same way as standard two-piece lids. They cost considerably more but last for several years, making the investment worth the initial upfront cost. If you plan to use these lids, be aware that their method of use is slightly different from traditional lids. Be extremely vigilant in following the manufacturer's guidelines to avoid widespread seal failure. The manufacturers are very helpful in instructing you on how their products work, so don't be afraid to give them a call.

Once you've purchased a few cases of canning jars, you will have enough rings that you probably won't need more unless you are giving your canned foods away as gifts. The rings are entirely reusable and are typically removed from the jars after canning to prevent them from rusting. If you do need more rings, you can purchase rings and lids together in one box.

There are numerous types of canning lids and jars sold predominantly online, including ones with lids made from glass. Typically expensive and not particularly practical for everyday use due to cost, they are nice for gift giving.

FROM THE MASTERS

JOSHUA RICKETT, CO-OWNER OF CECEILIA'S GARDENS
http://ceceiliascellar.com

There is no denying that canning is a lot of work. Seeking out fresh, organic produce, cleaning and processing all of those vegetables, and standing over a boiling crock of steam for hours—it's definitely a lot of work. But the delicious results make it all worth it. You will never find the same quality of taste and ingredients in a store-bought canned good as you would in the jars you put up at home. Sure, home canning takes time, but don't most good things in life require a little effort?

When I first started preserving food, I was canning everything in a water bath. I had no issues with my jams, but when I tried canning pickles, I ran into problems. Heat isn't great for most pickles, which is why commercial canners use pickling lime or alum to harden the cucumbers. This allows their pickles to stay crisp even when processed with lots of heat. Well, I didn't know this, so my first batch of pickles turned into sour cucumber soup. Yum. I wasn't discouraged, though, and learned from my mistakes. Now Ceceilia's Gardens produces crispy pickles by making them without heat, delivering crunchy textures without the need for chemical additives.

Developing new canned products using interesting or unusual ingredients can be a fun and creative outlet, but you want to do it safely. The main cause for concern when changing a tested recipe is the acidity. It's fine to try different amounts of herbs and spices in your homemade pickles, but don't adjust the vinegar or salt ratios. If you do, start with a small batch and test the acidity with a pH meter. (You will have to puree the contents in order to take a reading.) If the pH is below 4.6, then the batch is safe to can.

At Ceceilia's Gardens, some of our best preserves start out as experiments. Our 2015 Good Food Award winner, the Spicy Cardamom Pickles, is a great example. When developing that pickle, I had my brine set but no idea of what spices I wanted to use. So I basically closed my eyes and grabbed what I could. The results proved to be an award-winning bestseller.

SPECIALTY TOOLS. Two really helpful specialized canning tools are a *jar lifter* and a *wide-mouth funnel*.

- The jar lifter, slightly different than typical tongs, is curved to fit the shape of the jar and padded to minimize breakage. This tool, or something similar, is essential to lower and lift jars to and from the hot canner.
- The wide-mouth funnel makes filling jars a breeze, prevents you from making a mess, and helps the rims of the jars stay relatively clean while filling. A wide-mouth funnel is not a necessity to canning; it just makes doing so a lot simpler.

It is also helpful to have an **assortment of measuring cups** on hand. Heat-proof measuring cups, like those made by Pyrex, can be very helpful. A good set of stainless-steel or plastic measuring cups for measuring dry ingredients is equally as useful. You will also need an assortment of **nonreactive bowls** in various sizes for mixing ingredients.

OTHER EQUIPMENT

A few additional tools to have on hand include:

- **Kitchen scale.** This is a useful tool if you do any regular canning. With it you can accurately measure ingredients. A kitchen scale is inexpensive, typically around $20, and usually runs on standard batteries.
- **Candy thermometer.** Another important tool for jam and jelly making. Not every recipe requires this, but when making jams and jellies without added pectin, it is particularly helpful to monitor cooking temperatures to determine set. While not vital, it makes the task easier. If you don't have one, see page 32 to determine when your jam or jelly will set.

ESSENTIAL INGREDIENTS

Canning is a bit of both art and science. For the best results, it's critical to adhere to recipes as written. Once you master the basics, then you can put your creative talents to work. Ingredients are one key to successful canning. Using the proper ingredients called for in recipes increases the likelihood of success and ensures your food's safety.

SALT

Salt is used in many recipes to add flavor or, as with fermented pickles, aid in the fermentation process. Fine, granulated canning and pickling salt is the best option. This type of salt contains no added fillers to prevent clumping, which can leave an undesirable cloudy haze in your jars of canned foods. Sea salt can also be used when it is pure and contains no fillers. Avoid any colored sea salts. These can cause undesirable results when pickling. While many people prefer to use kosher salt, heating is often required to dissolve the salt's larger crystals in water (and then the water has to be cooled), adding both time and additional steps to the process. With this in mind, if you don't mind these extra steps, kosher salt can be used. Canning and pickling salt, sea salt, and kosher salt can be found in many grocery stores and specialty stores, or they can be ordered online.

VINEGAR

The recipes in *DIY Canning* call for several types of vinegar. Whichever kind you use, it is important that it is *5 percent acetic acid.* The amount of acid in vinegar is included on the label. Check the label, as not all vinegars are the same. Because their acidity can vary widely, do not use homemade vinegars for canning.

Note: Do not decrease the amount of vinegar in any recipe. This can lead to a product that is not correctly acidified for safety. Additionally, do not boil vinegar-based pickling liquids beyond the times stated in this book. This can decrease the amount of acetic acid in the mixture. Follow directions closely regarding the boiling of pickling liquid.

SUGAR

When sugar is called for in a recipe, granulated sugar is fine. You can decide whether you prefer standard granulated sugar, cane sugar, or organic sugar. However, do *not* substitute artificial sweeteners, as they do not hold up well to heat processing.

WATER

When water is needed, you can use filtered water or tap water in most cases. If your tap water tastes good and does not contain a large amount of chlorine or minerals, it is generally fine for the recipes here.

For hard water that leaves deposits in your sinks or toilet, you need to take an extra step to use it. Boil a large pot of water and then let it sit for 24 hours. Remove any scum from the surface and carefully transfer the water to another container, being careful to avoid disturbing the sediment on the bottom.

Chlorine can also be a problem, especially if you are fermenting. If you are using public water, it's a good practice to boil it for two minutes and allow it to cool before using, to eliminate any chlorine.

PECTIN

Pectin is used in many jam and jelly recipes. This naturally occurring material, found in the greatest quantities in underripe fruit, allows the jams and jellies to develop their firm texture. In some recipes, pectin is not used as the fruits have enough natural pectin to make jam easily. Before pectin was commercially made, this is how all jams were made. Pectin is effective in speeding the process and is available in liquid, powder, and low-sugar varieties. Follow the recipe's directions for the type of pectin used, as the methods for using each vary.

SPOTLIGHT ON PECTIN

Before the availability of commercially produced pectin, home jam makers relied on heat and a fruit's natural pectin to create jams and jellies with a thickened texture. Pectin, naturally used by fruits to build cell walls, works by forming invisible strands that lock moisture in when the pectin is dissolved and cooled to create a thickened finished product.

Some fruits naturally high in pectin include apples, blackberries, gooseberries, crabapples, cranberries, grapes, plums, and quince, as well as citrus fruit peels. For this reason, one or more of these fruits or their juices are sometimes used in small quantities without added pectin to achieve gelling.

In all fruits, pectin is highest when the fruit is underripe. This is why some recipes advise using up to one-quarter of underripe fruit to enable easier thickening. It is necessary to keep this ratio in check, though, as too much underripe fruit can adversely affect the flavor of the finished product.

Some fruits, such as apricots, blueberries, cherries, peaches, pears, raspberries, and strawberries, are low in natural pectin. These are good choices to use with commercially produced pectin when making into jams and jellies. Sold under the Certo and Sure-Jell brands, these pectins are derived from apples and/or citrus peels.

When using commercial pectins, do not reduce the sugar in a recipe unless specifically directed to do so. The pectin needs the sugar to react correctly with the fruit in order to gel. Also, with commercial pectin, use fully ripened fruit as you do not want additional pectin in the recipe from any underripe fruit.

There are some low-sugar pectins on the market, which allow you to change the standard ratio of sugar to fruit considerably. To make the most significantly low-sugar jams, Pomona's Pectin is the best option. When using this in a recipe, such as the low-sugar Golden Summer Conserve (see page 81), do not substitute another low-sugar pectin. Most are not formulated to use as little sugar as this type of pectin does. Pomona's Pectin can be found at specialty retailers or ordered online.

Commercially produced pectin is available in two main varieties: powdered and liquid. Powdered pectin has a longer shelf life, so stock up if you find a sale. When buying a large quantity, check the "use by" date on the box, as the gelling ability diminishes over time.

Powdered pectin is added to recipes at the same time as the fruit, while liquid pectin is added at the end of cooking after the jam or jelly is removed from the heat. Take special note of these differences in process, especially when adapting a recipe to use a different type of pectin.

When using pectin, your results will typically be more consistent than when relying on natural fruit pectin alone. Either way, though, there is always the chance of set failure when making jams and jellies. If this happens, you can either cook the product again to try to correct the problem, or simply call them syrups and start cooking those pancakes and waffles.

To avoid commercial pectin altogether, you can use a homemade pectin stock. Made from Granny Smith apples, which have high levels of pectin, this stock can be used in place of commercial pectin. To use pectin stock in jams and jellies, the suggested ratio of stock to fruit or fruit purée is about ⅔ cup pectin stock to 4 cups prepared fruit.

HOMEMADE PECTIN STOCK

MAKES 4 HALF-PINT JARS

WATER-BATH CANNING

Apples are extremely subtle and nearly flavorless when added to other preserves. Don't worry about removing the seeds; leaving them in during cooking adds pectin to the broth. The strength of homemade pectin may not be as consistent as commercial pectin, so test the preserves while cooking and make any necessary adjustments.

PREP TIME: 10 minutes
COOK TIME: 35 minutes, plus 12 hours draining time
PROCESSING TIME: 5 minutes
TOTAL TIME: 12 hours, 50 minutes

- 3½ pounds Granny Smith apples, coarsely chopped (peeling and coring not needed)
- 4 cups water
- 1 tablespoon freshly squeezed lemon juice
- Rubbing alcohol, for testing gel

DAY 1

1. In a preserving pot (see page 16) set over medium-high heat, combine the apples, water, and lemon juice. Bring to a boil. Reduce the heat to medium. Cover the pot. Cook, stirring occasionally, until the apples are very tender, 25 to 30 minutes.

2. Line a colander with a couple layers of cheesecloth and put a bowl underneath it. Pour the apple mixture into the colander and let the juice drip, without disturbing the apples, until most of the liquid has drained into the bowl, about 12 hours or overnight. Discard the apples and reserve the juice.

DAY 2

1. Prepare a hot water bath (see page 30). Place the jars in it to keep warm. Wash the lids and rings in hot, soapy water, and set aside.

2. In a medium saucepan, bring about 5 cups of the juice to a simmer over medium-high heat. Cook for about 5 minutes, or until reduced by about one-fifth.

3. Test the pectin stock to determine if it sets (see page 24). If necessary, continue to reduce and retest.

4. Ladle the stock into the prepared jars, leaving ½ inch of headspace. Use a nonmetallic utensil to release any air bubbles. Wipe the rims clean and seal with the lids and rings.

Continued

HOMEMADE PECTIN STOCK

CONTINUED

5. Process in a hot water bath (see page 31) for 5 minutes. Turn off the heat and let the jars rest in the water bath for 10 minutes.

6. Carefully remove the jars from the hot water canner. Set on a countertop to cool for 12 hours.

7. Check the lids for proper seals (see page 32). If the lids don't pop back when pressed down, you can remove the rings, wipe the jars, label them, and transfer to a cupboard or pantry. The rings may be replaced on the jars to help keep the lids in place after opening.

8. Refrigerate any jars that didn't seal properly, and use within 3 weeks. Unopened jars will last in the cupboard for 12 months. Once opened, refrigerate and consume within 3 weeks.

TESTING FOR PECTIN GEL

To test the pectin stock, spoon about 2 teaspoons into a shallow dish. Add about 2 tablespoons of rubbing alcohol and swirl together. If the stock forms a few large clumps, it is strong enough. If it forms a lot of small clumps, it needs to cook a little longer. Discard the test sample, as rubbing alcohol is poisonous. If necessary, return the remaining stock to the heat, simmer until it is reduced by about one-fourth, and test again. Continue reducing and testing until the pectin sets properly.

A PLETHORA OF PRODUCE

PRODUCE PURCHASE GUIDE

Ripe, fresh produce is what you want for your canning projects. Produce from a grocery store is fine, but you will find better quality, and better prices, at a farmers' market or produce store selling local, seasonal fruits and vegetables. You don't really want to use items hanging around for weeks, as is often the case in larger grocery stores.

Buying direct from farms has its advantages. You get to know local farmers and get a peek into their lives and livelihoods. Buying organic is always best, for your health and the environment, but many small farms are not able to gain organic certification for a number of reasons. Many farmers may farm organically, or close to it. Finding these resources may allow you to buy produce that is organic, but not labeled as such, for considerably less than you would otherwise. Talk with the local farmers about their pest management programs and ease any concerns you may have about buying from them.

Consider buying large quantities of fruits or vegetables to can a number of recipes at once. Buying in bulk can definitely be cheaper, but just make sure you have room for storage and ample time to process the food. Apples, tomatoes, beans, peas, grapes, and many other types of produce can be purchased in 20-pound boxes for considerable discounts. If you have a basement or cool area in your house, you can store these for a couple days as you work through them. Other items like cucumbers should be processed within a day or two of picking for best results. Stock up when you can, but be realistic about how much time you have for canning before you purchase too much.

Applesauce, pectin stock, and apple and pear butters are great ways to use slightly overripe and even banged-up fruits. For most other projects, top-quality, ripe, and blemish-free fruits and vegetables are key. If a peach, plum, tomato, or nectarine has a dark spot, that's okay. Just cut it away before canning to prevent off flavors in your finished products.

It is important to understand the pH of foods before beginning any canning project, particularly if you are not following a specific recipe. While fruits like peaches, pears, and plums can be interchangeable in some recipes, other fruits such as Asian pears and white peaches are considered low acid and must be acidified when canned. Before you start improvising and substituting ingredients, check Appendix B: pH Ranges of Common Foods (see page 234) to make informed decisions.

PRODUCE WEIGHT/ VOLUME/YIELD GUIDE

Some recipes in this book use weight (what an ingredient actually weighs, e.g., 1 pound), while others use volume (how much space an ingredient takes up, e.g., 1 cup) as the measurement for quantities of fruits, vegetables, and meats. Using weight is the most accurate way to get consistency in processing. However, volume measurements have advantages, too. This book uses the measurement most appropriate for the recipe.

The difference between these two measuring methods can create some variables. While weight is an accurate measurement, using a volume measurement is often the easiest way to maintain consistency in a product like salsa where you are removing the tomatoes' seeds, liquid, skins, and cores..

When weight is used, actually weigh the produce. Do not estimate, as this can cause problems, especially in low-acid foods that are acidified to enable processing in a water-bath canner. If you do not have a kitchen scale, weigh the produce and note its weight when purchasing.

FOUR SEASONS OF FOOD

SPRING

Spring gives us the first fresh fruits and vegetables of the year. Toward the end of the season, strawberries emerge and, after the long wait, it is difficult to have just one. Thankfully, by the time you think you can't eat any more, their short season is over and summer's bounty awaits.

- Asparagus
- Rhubarb
- Snap peas
- Spinach
- Strawberries

SUMMER

This is the glory time for canners. All the prized fruits and vegetables appear now. There is abundant selection at the grocery store, as well as farmers' markets and produce stands. This is the time to tackle all those projects you have earmarked for the year.

- Apricots
- Artichokes
- Beans
- Bell peppers
- Blackberries
- Blueberries
- Boysenberries
- Cherries
- Collard greens
- Cucumbers
- Hot peppers
- Nectarines
- Peaches
- Plums
- Raspberries
- Summer squash
- Tomatoes
- Watermelon
- Zucchini

FALL

Like nature does in fall, canning season also winds down. There are plenty of fresh fruits still to put up for winter, but the showing of vegetables begins to dwindle. Spend a bit more time by the stove, as temperatures begin to decline, and put up the last of the apples, grapes, and pears now.

- Apples
- Cabbage
- Cranberries
- Figs
- Grapes
- Greens
- Pears
- Pumpkin
- Winter squash

WINTER

During winter, very little fresh, locally grown produce appears. Citrus fruits are the star of the season, as they are sweetest and juiciest at this time. Focus on putting up dried beans, soups, and stews early in the season to enjoy through the long, dark days of winter. Look through your canning books during this time and dream about the coming year.

- Cabbage
- Grapefruit
- Kumquats
- Oranges
- Quince

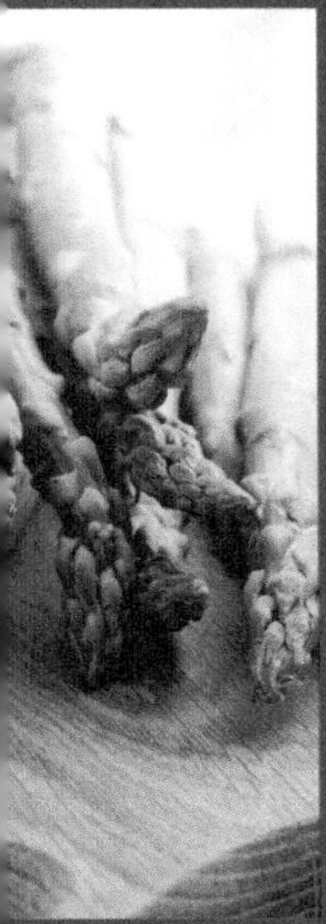

2

YOUR FIRST BATCHES

Now that you're equipped with the necessary supplies and a "can do" attitude, you're ready to jump in full force and begin canning. The following two recipes are for practice. They will guide you through the basics of these two types of canning with step-by-step instructions. Once you master these simple projects, you're ready to proceed to any of the recipes in the book.

The first covers water-bath canning and uses a simple strawberry jam recipe. Of the many types of preserves out there, jams are one of the easiest to make. Fruit is cooked with sugar in a deep pot with some lemon juice to help it set. Jams like the recipe on the next page are usually prepared using the hot-pack method, meaning the ingredients are cooked and hot when ladled into jars, before being processed in a hot water bath. Nearly any fruit can be turned into jam, but strawberries are one of the easiest and most classic ingredients to work with. Your reward will be six jars of ruby-red jam—perfect for homemade scones, muffins, or a thick slice of toast.

The second recipe covers pressure canning and uses green beans to start. No matter whether this is your first time pressure canning or you have done it many times before, closely following these directions will help you create safely canned food. Processing times vary, but these steps apply to any pressure canning project you undertake.

STRAWBERRY JAM

MAKES 6 HALF-PINT JARS

WATER-BATH CANNING

Strawberry jam is a simple jam made from fresh berries crushed together with sugar and cooked until thick and spreadable. This small-batch recipe is perfect for learning and perfecting your jam-making skills. If you want to skip the canning step (but that defeats the purpose), pack the jam in containers and freeze. Or make a batch each way!

PREP TIME: 15 minutes
COOK TIME: 15 minutes
PROCESSING TIME: 10 minutes
TOTAL TIME: 40 minutes

- 2 pounds fresh whole, ripe strawberries, hulled and halved (about 2 quarts)
- 2 pounds (4 cups) sugar
- 1 tablespoon freshly squeezed lemon juice

1. Wash the jars, lids, and rings in hot soapy water. As you do this, inspect the jars to ensure they are free of chips or cracks, paying special attention to the rims. Be sure the rings are not bent or rusty. If you have a new box of lids purchased during 2014 or later, they do not require heating and you can set them aside with the rings as they dry.

2. If you have an older box of lids purchased before 2014, they need to be heated to soften the sealing compound. To do so, place them in a saucepot filled with water and lightly simmer until they are needed. Do not boil them, as this can negatively affect the sealing compound.

3. Fill the water-bath canner halfway with water and place it on the stove. Insert the rack of jars into the canner (see fig. A). Bring the water to a gentle simmer and keep it there until ready to use the canner.

4. Into a large mixing bowl, measure the sugar and set aside.

5. In a preserving pot (see page 16), crush the berries well using clean hands or a potato masher. Add the lemon juice and sugar. Bring to a boil over medium heat, stirring occasionally to keep the jam from scorching.

6. When the jam reaches a full rolling boil, it will foam. Stir constantly to keep the jam from boiling over or scorching. Boil for 10 to 15 minutes, or until the jam reaches the gel stage, testing for gel after 5 minutes (see instructions following).

A

B

C

D

E

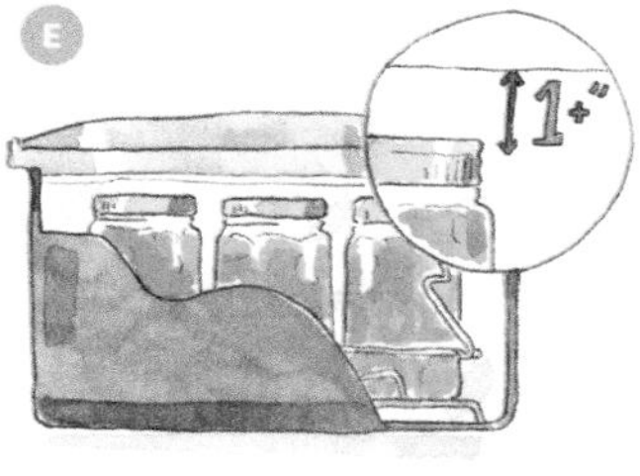

F

7. Remove the pot from the heat. Using a ladle, transfer the jam to the prepared jars, leaving ¼ inch of headspace (see fig. B). Use a nonmetallic utensil to remove any air bubbles by inserting the utensil along the side of the jar one or two times (see fig. C). In a food like jam, bubbles are unlikely to form, but it is good practice to do this as omitting to remove air bubbles can result in seal failure.

8. With a wet paper towel or a wet, clean washcloth, wipe the rims clean (see fig. D). There can be no pieces of food or residue along the rim, as this prevents the sealing compound from working properly.

9. Apply the lids with the sealing compound facing down, and screw on the rings until just tightened and there is resistance. Don't overtighten the rings, but ensure they are snugly in place.

10. Using a jar lifter, carefully lower the jars into the water-bath canner. Place the jars on opposite sides of the canner to balance them and prevent jars from tipping over. Once the jars are situated and the rack is lowered, be sure the water covers the jars by 2 inches. If not, add hot water to the canner(see fig.E).

11. Cover the canner and increase the heat to medium-high to bring the water to a rolling boil. Process the jars in the hot water bath for 10 minutes. Start timing once the water is at a full rolling boil. If necessary, refer to Appendix A: Altitude Adjustments (see page 233) to make adjustments to the processing time based on your altitude.

12. When the time is up, turn off the heat, carefully remove the top of the canner, and let the jars rest in the water bath for 10 minutes.

Continued

STRAWBERRY JAM
CONTINUED

13. Carefully remove the jars from the hot water canner and place them on a covered surface, such as a towel or cutting board (see fig. F). Placing jars on an exposed counter can cause a quick change in temperature, which can result in breakage. Be sure to leave at least 1 inch of space between the jars to allow for air circulation. Do not tighten the lids or adjust the jars in any way. Allow the jars 12 hours to cool and seal.

IS IT JAM YET?

When making jam without added pectin, place a couple small plates in the freezer before you begin. When you think the jam is ready to test, pull the pot from the heat and use a clean spoon to remove some jam. Pull out one of the plates, add the jam, and put it back in the freezer to cool for a minute, then taste. If you like the flavor and consistency, it's done.

Another test is to spoon a small amount of jam onto a cool surface and let it cool to room temperature. If you run your finger through the cooled jam, the skin should wrinkle and your finger should leave an imprint in the jam. If the jam doesn't pass these gel tests, return it to the heat and continue to boil, testing the jam every two or three minutes until it is done.

14. Wash and dry the canner well for its next use. Skipping this step contributes to the quick decline of enameled water-bath canners.

15. Test the seal on the jars by pushing on the center of each lid. Remove the rings from the jars and lift them by the lid. The lid should stay attached to the jar. If the jars pass these two tests, they are properly sealed. Wipe each jar with a clean, damp cloth to remove any residue that may remain around the rim or threads of the jar.

16. If the lid pops back up after being pressed, refrigerate those jars and use within 4 weeks. Properly sealed jars will keep in a cupboard or pantry for up to 1 year. Once opened, refrigerate and use within 4 weeks. Be sure to label the jars with the contents and date of processing.

TRY INSTEAD

You can replace some or all of the strawberries with blueberries, raspberries, currants, gooseberries, boysenberries, marionberries, or lingonberries. When the growing season changes, replace the berries with an equal weight of peaches, plums, apricots, or cherries. For other fruits, consult a good conversion table (see page 238) to find out how much fresh fruit you need.

GREEN BEANS

MAKES 6 PINT JARS

PRESSURE CANNING, LOW-SODIUM

Green beans are one of the easiest foods to can. In the summer, you can find them for sale by the box or you can simply grow these prolific vegetables in a sunny spot in your garden. This recipe uses the raw-packed method, making it super quick to get the beans from sink to jar.

PREP TIME: 15 minutes
COOK TIME: 0
PROCESSING TIME: 20 minutes
TOTAL TIME: 35 minutes

6 pounds green beans, washed, ends trimmed, and snapped or cut into 1-inch segments
Water
3 teaspoons salt, divided (optional)

1. Before beginning, inspect all your jars to ensure they do not have any chips or cracks that can lead to breakage. Examine the rims of the jars to ensure they are flat and even. Look at the lids to ensure the sealing compound goes all the way around it; confirm the rings are free of rust and dents.

2. Prepare the jars, lids, and rings for canning by washing them in hot, soapy water. If you have a new box of lids purchased during 2014 or later, they do not require heating and you can set them aside with the rings as they dry.

3. If you have an older box of lids purchased *before* 2014, they need to be heated to soften the sealing compound. To do so, place them in a saucepot filled with water and lightly simmer until they are needed. Do not boil them, as this can negatively affect the sealing compound.

4. Inspect your pressure canner to confirm it is in working order. Inspect the gasket to make sure it is free of cracks and still fits well. Use a pipe cleaner to clean the vent pipe and clear it of debris. Consult your canner's user guide for additional information on maintenance and inspection for your particular canner. Once you confirm that the canner is in good shape, place the rack in it and add 3 to 4 inches of water.

5. Fill the jars with a couple inches of water so they do not float, and place them in the canner (see fig. A). Bring the water to a simmer until ready to fill the jars. *Do not boil the water.*

Continued

GREEN BEANS
CONTINUED

6. Bring a separate large pot of water to a boil on the stove.

7. Carefully remove the jars from the canner, empty them into the sink, and place them on a cutting board on a nearby countertop.

8. Pack the beans tightly into the empty jars, leaving 1 inch of headspace. If desired, add ½ teaspoon of salt to each jar.

9. Using a wide-mouth funnel to cover the first jar, ladle in the boiling water. Continue until all the jars are full, with 1 inch of headspace left in each (see fig. B). In general, for most low-acid foods you will leave 1 inch of headspace.

10. Use a nonmetallic utensil, such as an air bubble remover or a plastic knife, to remove any air bubbles by running it along the sides of the jar. Do not skip this step even if there are no visible air bubbles, as these can cause seal failure and breakage. Insert the tool two or three times in different spots along the inside of the jar for best results.

11. Use a wet paper towel or wet, clean dishtowel to clean the rims of the jars. There should be nothing along the rim of the jar when you apply the lids and rings, as this can prevent proper sealing.

12. Center the lids on the jars with the sealing compound facing down, and affix them with the rings. Screw the rings on until you have resistance. Avoid overtightening the rings, but also avoid undertightening them. They should be snugly fixed in place.

13. Using a jar lifter, carefully place the jars in the canner. Once the jars are in place, close the canner and lock its lid in place.

14. Turn the heat to medium-high. Continue heating the canner until steam is steadily coming out of the vent pipe (see fig. C). *The pressure regulator should not be in place at this time*. Once the steam begins exiting in a steady stream, start a timer for 10 minutes.

15. When the time is up, place the pressure regulator on the vent pipe. Turn the heat up to high and watch as the pressure increases. Once the correct pressure (10 psi on a weighted gauge or 11 psi on a dial gauge) is reached, lower the heat slightly to maintain that pressure. If you live at an elevation higher than 1,000 feet, consult Appendix A: Altitude Adjustments (see page 233) for the correct pressure for your location.

16. Set a timer for 20 minutes to process the beans. Make adjustments to the temperature, as needed, to maintain a steady pressure. If the pressure drops, you will need to bring the pressure back up and start the timing again from the beginning to ensure it is safely processed. Make slight adjustments, instead of large ones, to maintain even pressure.

17. When the time is up, turn the burner off and move the canner to a cool burner. *Do not remove the gauge or attempt to open the canner at this time.* Allow the canner to reach zero pressure on its own. Once it reads 0, let it rest for another 5 minutes to ensure safely removing the lid. When you are ready to remove the lid, turn it away from your face to prevent a steam burn.

18. Using a jar lifter, carefully remove the jars from the canner and place them on a nearby cutting board or kitchen towel. Leave at least 1 inch of space between the jars so air is able to circulate freely. Let the jars cool on their own and do not adjust the rings.

19. After 12 hours of resting, check that the lids are properly sealed (see fig. D). Most often, you can see whether the jar is sealed if the center dome of the lid is popped down (see fig. E). Remove the rings from the jars and then lift each jar by its lid to determine a proper seal. The lids should not move. If any jars have not sealed, refrigerate them and consume within several days. If a large amount did not seal, they can be reprocessed using new lids.

20. Use a damp cloth to wipe down the jars. Label and date the beans so you can keep track of what to eat first.

21. Store the jars in a cool, dry, and dark location for up to 12 months.

EVALUATING YOUR PROCESS AND PRODUCT WORKSHEET

FACTORS AFFECTING RECIPE OUTCOME RECOMMENDATIONS	CONDITIONS DURING RECIPE EXECUTION	NOTES FOR NEXT TIME
Quality/ripeness of fruit Use ripe berries because of their higher acid and pectin percentage (see page 21 for more information about pectin).		
Cooking time Test for gel throughout the cooking process at regular intervals to assess doneness. Apply as many tests for doneness as possible, and rely on your own preferences to determine when it is done.		
Cooking temperature Maintain a full, rolling boil.		
Batch size Use a cooking time based on quantities specified in the recipe.		
Processing time 10 minutes, adjusted for altitude.		
Amount of sugar Equal parts sugar and fruit by weight.		
Amount of acid 1 tablespoon freshly squeezed lemon juice added at the start of cooking time to assist gelling.		
Color Crush fruit rather than dicing, slicing, or puréeing it.		
Texture Test for a gel after 5 minutes of boiling time and every 3 to 4 minutes thereafter, since that is more accurate than simply cooking for a set time. Leave the jars undisturbed for 12 hours after processing so the gel is not disturbed.		

EVALUATING YOUR PROCESS AND PRODUCT

Barring any real disasters, like burning the jam or skipping the processing step, your finished product should be great. But even seasoned food preservers know some batches are better than others when it comes to achieving the perfect flavor, texture, or color. The best way to improve is by learning from your experiences.

Take time to evaluate your results, making notes on what happened as opposed to what the recipe instructed. Keep in mind that a variety of factors contribute to different results. These can include the ripeness of ingredients, the quality of your water, and the humidity in your kitchen. By taking the time to make notes regarding your process, ingredients used, and the final outcome, you can improve your results over time.

Answer the following questions about your jam:

- Is my jam spreadable, runny, or too thick?
- Is my jam a brilliant color, a little washed out, or a little dark?
- Does my jam taste like strawberries?

Evaluate your outcome against recipe recommendations and make notes for future batches in the table on the opposite page.

LOW-SODIUM AND LOW-SUGAR CANNING

For some people, adapting recipes to be lower in sugar or sodium may be desired for health or taste reasons. In some recipes this can be completely fine to do, while in others, it is not.

Salt in canning is typically used for flavor, not its preservative quality. While pickles require a decent amount of salt to be successful, other canned vegetables can be made safely without salt, or with reduced amounts, as desired.

The biggest benefit of holding the salt when making canned vegetables, meats, and fish comes when these are used as part of a larger dish, as opposed to being eaten on their own. This way, you can precisely control the amount of salt in the finished dish. If you will be eating the item on its own, however, salt can add welcome flavor. For specific tips on where to reduce salt, keep an eye out for "low-sodium preparation tips" at the end of recipes where this is an option.

Sugar is a bit trickier to reduce in many canned foods, most notably jams and jellies. Depending on the process you use to make jam (powdered pectin, liquid pectin, no added pectin), changing the amounts of sugar in a recipe can greatly affect the jam set. Closely follow these recipes as is, and do not alter the amount of sugar, unless the recipe includes a "low-sugar preparation tip."

For other items, such as canned whole fruits, the sugar syrup can be replaced with water to save on calories. Canning fruits in water is perfectly safe. However, when canned in a sugar syrup, even a very light one, the fruits tend to plump a bit and have a better flavor. Depending on how you will use the fruit, this may or may not be an issue.

TROUBLESHOOTING TIPS

As with any cooking project, sometimes things just don't work out quite right. Here are some of the most common problems, what causes them, and how to fix them the next time.

JAM DIDN'T SET

There are many factors that can affect whether a jam sets properly. If you use commercial pectin, process can play a large role. Using the correct amount of sugar and following the steps in proper order, including using a timer, are important to achieving set. If you made a jam or jelly without pectin, it is important to follow the testing procedures (see page 32) to create a thickened jam or jelly. While cooking times are outlined for several recipes, variables such as your range, the type of pot being used, humidity, and your fruit's moisture can play a role in the set of your jams and jellies. Use your best judgment when cooking these preserves, and do not rely simply on the suggested times.

JARS DIDN'T SEAL

There are many reasons that jars do not seal. The most common one is that the rims were not cleaned properly. Use a wet cloth to wipe the rims perfectly clean before applying the lids. Also, don't forget (or skip) the step to remove air bubbles in the food before sealing the jars. Skipping this can also create seal failure. Always inspect the lids before use to ensure they have sealing compound all the way around, as every once in a while you will find one that doesn't. If this occurs, discard it. For jars that didn't seal properly, you can reheat their contents back to the original packing temperature and process them again in the canner.

JAR BREAKAGE

The most common reason that jars break is they are placed in the canner when the water is too hot and the contents of the jar are too cool. This is most common when cold-packing foods. To avoid this, the water in the canner should just simmer, not boil, when the jars are added. Additionally, the liquid going into the jars must be heated adequately before filling them. Even raw-packed foods must have a boiling liquid covering them. The next time you pack these foods, work on one jar at a time, adding it back to the canner as you go so it gets back into the canner before the liquid cools too much.

FROM THE MASTERS

BRADLEY BENNETT, FOUNDER/PRINCIPAL PICKLE OF PACIFIC PICKLE WORKS
www.pacificpickleworks.com

I started out by making pickles every fall as a hobby and giving them away as holiday gifts. I would tweak the balance of vinegar, salt, and sugar in the brine of each batch, and eventually, the demand for my pickles grew until I could no longer keep up. With the encouragement of friends and family, I started Pacific Pickle Works in 2010 as a side business, selling my products in just a few stores around town. Within a couple of years there was enough business to let me leave my full time job as a software engineer and focus on the pickle business full time. Using local and organic produce grown in California, we have since perfected a "West Coast" style of spicy pickles that has won over fans both in and out of the state.

The secret to a successful pickle recipe is more than just the brine—the quality of the vegetables you choose is also very important. Often people will get rid of extra produce by pickling it, but if you start with inferior produce, expect an inferior result. We won the 2015 Good Food Award for our Jalabeaños (spicy pickled green beans) because the ingredients we use are the finest available. Organic and locally grown, the green beans come from only one farm in Santa Barbara and are purchased seasonally at the height of freshness. We pickle them the day after they're harvested to capture the maximum amount of flavor and texture in the jar. We're picky about our cucumbers, too; when we buy cucumbers, we don't use the big old ones with mushy insides and loose seeds. We choose young, firm cucumbers that give a satisfying crunch after they're pickled.

No two vegetables are the same when it comes to the way they should be pickled. In making your pickles, you may want to emphasize certain characteristics of the flavors by using different spices and adjusting the intensity of sweetness or sourness. When it comes to texture, every product we create spends a different amount of time in the canner because we want the texture experience to be different for each type of pickle. Be creative with your pickles. They don't need to be overly complex—sometimes the simplest pickle can be the most delicious!

INCORRECT YIELDS

Similar to cooking times, yields listed can be variable. Some years are rainier than others, causing fruits and vegetables to swell with water, which evaporates during cooking, resulting in a lower yield. Conversely, drier years can result in denser fruits and vegetables that have more concentrated sugars, resulting in higher yields. If you end up with extra, refrigerate it for immediate use. Having some smaller jars on hand is helpful when a recipe comes up a little short.

FOOD SPOILAGE

Surprisingly, food spoilage when canning is actually quite rare. However, be vigilant whenever using home-canned foods to ensure their safety. Before opening a can of food, look at it. Does anything look off? Is the lid bulging, or does it have a good-quality seal? If bubbles are moving or mold is present on the surface of the food, it is bad and should be discarded. Remove the top and smell the food. Are any odors present? Are there any other signs of spoilage such as food sputtering out of the jar or mold growing on the inside of the lid? These are all signs of spoilage. If the food is spoiled, or you suspect spoilage, do *not* taste it to confirm. Instead, replace the lid on the jar and place it in a pot of water. Boil the jar and contents for 30 minutes, cool, and then discard the food in the garbage. Be sure to thoroughly wash and disinfect the work area, tools, and utensils used, and your hands after handling spoiled food.

HEIRLOOM RECIPES

Many people have amassed collections of canning recipes passed from generation to generation. However, based on today's knowledge of food safety coming from extensive research and testing of food preservation recipes and methods, these may not all be deemed safe. Practice caution when using these recipes. Practices have changed quite a bit over the last century.

It is important to follow modern methods, as they have evolved with safety in mind. The fact that your grandmother did something one way and no one got sick does not make it a safe practice. After all, the ultimate goal is to feed our families safely and healthily.

For concerns about the safety of a particular recipe, contact your local cooperative extension office. The cooperative extension system is a nationwide network of U.S. state and regional offices that provide useful, practical, research-based information to agricultural producers, consumers, youth, and other folks who want to educate themselves about food and agriculture. They can often point you in the correct direction. Otherwise, use modern processing specifications for acidifying foods. Tomatoes, for example, are considered by many to be a high-acid food and therefore not acidified in many heirloom recipes. However, by today's standards tomatoes should be acidified. The pH of tomatoes varies greatly by variety. With the recent surge in heirloom tomatoes, which have less acid than other types, it is more important than ever to acidify them.

THE RECIPES II

3

JAMS, JELLIES, MARMALADES & PRESERVES

These are the crown jewels of the canning world, and with good reason: they are fantastic when homemade. Many of the following recipes use pectin, while others do not. Some include spices and herbs, and others offer a simple fruit-forward flavor. Combining art, science, and the variability of nature, fruit spreads can be slightly different each batch, giving them their unique character.

BLACKBERRY AND APPLE JAM

MAKES 5 HALF-PINT JARS

WATER-BATH CANNING

This is a classic example of how to make the most of the flurry of fruit that fills markets each fall. Blackberry seeds can be irritating to eat, so here you'll strain the jam. Skip that step if you like the added crunch of the seeds.

PREP TIME: 15 minutes
COOK TIME: 35 minutes
PROCESSING TIME: 10 minutes
TOTAL TIME: 1 hour

- 2 large cooking apples, cored and thinly sliced, cores reserved
- 3 pounds fresh blackberries
- 5 cups sugar
- 3 tablespoons freshly squeezed lemon juice
- 2 to 3 tablespoons blackberry or raspberry cordial, or liqueur (optional)

1. Prepare a hot water bath (see page 30). Place the jars in it to keep warm. Wash the lids and rings in hot, soapy water, and set aside.

2. Put the reserved apple cores in a piece of cheesecloth and tie the ends securely with kitchen twine into a sachet.

3. In a preserving pot or deep pot, combine the apple slices, blackberries, and the sachet. Cover the fruit with water. Bring to a simmer over medium heat and cook for about 10 minutes, stirring frequently, or until the fruit is very tender and starting to fall apart.

4. Remove the pot from the heat. Remove and discard the sachet.

5. Using a sieve or fine strainer, purée the fruit by passing it through into a clean pan.

6. Add the sugar, lemon juice, and cordial (if using). Return the mixture to a simmer over low heat.

7. Continue to cook, stirring often, for 20 to 25 minutes or until the jam gels and the mixture reaches 220°F, measured with a candy thermometer. Test for gel after 20 minutes (see page 32).

8. Ladle the jam into the prepared jars, leaving ¼ inch of headspace. Use a nonmetallic utensil to release any air bubbles. Wipe the rims clean and seal with the lids and rings.

9. Process the jars in a hot water bath (see page 31) for 10 minutes. Turn off the heat and let the jars rest in the water bath for 10 minutes.

10. Carefully remove the jars from the hot water canner. Set aside to cool for 12 hours.

11. Check the lids for proper seals (see page 32). Remove the rings, wipe the jars, label and date them, and transfer to a cupboard or pantry.

12. Refrigerate any jars that don't seal properly,, and use within 1 month. Properly sealed jars will last in the cupboard for 12 months. Once opened, refrigerate and consume within 1 month.

TRY INSTEAD

Ladling jam can be tricky, especially when hot. Instead of ladling the jam with a regular ladle, use a clean coffee mug to scoop the jam or jelly from the pan and transfer it to the jars. The squat design of a coffee cup gives you more control and helps you avoid a big mess to clean.

GINGERED NECTARINE JAM

MAKES 3 PINT JARS

WATER-BATH CANNING

Three different styles of ginger add a pleasant burn to this brilliant orange jam. For this recipe, it's best if the nectarines are ripe but still firm. If they are a little soft, you may want to increase the lemon juice by one teaspoon.

PREP TIME: 20 minutes
COOK TIME: 45 minutes
PROCESSING TIME: 10 minutes
TOTAL TIME: 1 hour, 15 minutes

2½ pounds nectarines, pitted, peeled, and chopped
1½ cups sugar
2 tablespoons freshly squeezed lemon juice
2 tablespoons minced candied ginger
1 tablespoon finely grated fresh ginger
2 teaspoons ground ginger

1. Prepare a hot water bath (see page 30). Place the jars in it to keep warm. Wash the lids and rings in hot, soapy water, and set aside.

2. In a preserving pot set over low heat, combine the nectarines, sugar, lemon juice, candied ginger, fresh ginger, and ground ginger. Bring to a simmer. Cook for 40 to 45 minutes, stirring often, or until the jam gels and the mixture reaches 220°F, measured with a candy thermometer. Test for gel after 40 minutes (see page 32).

3. Ladle the jam into the prepared jars, leaving ¼ inch of headspace. Use a nonmetallic utensil to release any air bubbles. Wipe the rims clean and seal with the lids and rings.

4. Process the jars in a hot water bath (see page 31) for 10 minutes. Turn off the heat and let the jars rest in the water bath for 10 minutes.

5. Carefully remove the jars from the hot water canner. Set aside to cool for 12 hours.

6. Check the lids for proper seals (see page 32). Remove the rings, wipe the jars, label and date them, and transfer to a cupboard or pantry.

7. Refrigerate any jars that don't seal properly, and use within 1 month. Properly sealed jars will last in the cupboard for 12 months. Once opened, refrigerate and consume within 1 month.

CLOSER LOOK

Candied ginger is a breeze to make and sure beats paying crazy amounts for this sweet and spicy treat. Peel and slice ginger and place it in a saucepan on the stove. Mix equal parts of sugar and water to create a syrup, and simmer the ginger in it for 30 minutes. Strain the ginger from the syrup. Lay it flat in a single layer on a drying sheet for about 5 hours, or until completely dry. Roll the pieces in sugar and you are done. If not using immediately, or you have extra, store it in an airtight container for 3 weeks.

RASPBERRY JAM

MAKES 5 HALF-PINT JARS

WATER-BATH CANNING

Raspberry jams and preserves are a common treat today. There was a time, however, especially throughout Eastern Europe and Russia, when this jam was prized as a cure-all and special treat to be savored only occasionally, perhaps stirred into a glass of hot tea. Whether raspberry jam has any real curative powers is a matter of debate. Who's to say that the taste of summer won't make you feel better?

PREP TIME: 5 minutes
COOK TIME: 20 minutes
PROCESSING TIME: 10 minutes
TOTAL TIME: 35 minutes

2¼ pounds whole fresh red raspberries
3½ cups sugar
⅓ to ½ cup freshly squeezed lemon juice, as needed

1. Prepare a hot water bath (see page 30). Place the jars in it to keep warm. Wash the lids and rings in hot, soapy water, and set aside.

2. In a preserving pot or a deep pot, combine the raspberries and sugar. With clean hands, a potato masher, or the back of a wooden spoon, mash the berries to release the juices. Taste the mixture and add lemon juice to taste.

3. Bring the mixture to a simmer over medium heat. Reduce the heat to low. Cook for 15 to 20 minutes, stirring often, or until the jam gels and the mixture reaches 220°F, measured with a candy thermometer. Test for gel after 5 minutes (see page 32).

4. Ladle the jam into the prepared jars, leaving ¼ inch of headspace. Use a nonmetallic utensil to release any air bubbles. Wipe the rims clean and seal with the lids and rings.

5. Process the jars in a hot water bath (see page 31) for 10 minutes. Turn off the heat and let the jars rest in the water bath for 10 minutes.

6. Carefully remove the jars from the hot water canner. Set aside to cool for 12 hours.

7. Check the lids for proper seals (see page 32). Remove the rings, wipe the jars, label and date them, and transfer to a cupboard or pantry.

8. Refrigerate any jars that don't seal properly, and use within 2 months. Properly sealed jars will last in the cupboard for 12 months. Once opened, refrigerate and consume within 2 months.

TRY INSTEAD

This recipe works with either fresh or frozen berries, and comes in handy if you have frozen berries to use before the coming year's harvest. If you use frozen berries, let them thaw partially, but not quite all the way.

FIGGY JAM

MAKES 3 PINT JARS

WATER-BATH CANNING, SEASONAL

This jam is quite thick. When it boils there's a chance it will splatter. Wear oven mitts to protect your hands and arms from burns. You need wide strips of lemon peel—not grated zest—for this recipe. Use a vegetable peeler to cut the strips from the lemon before juicing it.

PREP TIME: 20 minutes, plus 1 hour resting time
COOK TIME: 1 hour, 5 minutes
PROCESSING TIME: 10 minutes
TOTAL TIME: 2 hours, 35 minutes

3 pounds fresh figs, stemmed and cut into eighths
1 cup sugar, divided
¾ cup honey
½ cup brandy
Peel of 1 lemon
Juice of 1 lemon
1 teaspoon kosher salt
3 tablespoons light pectin

1. In a preserving pot or deep saucepot, combine the figs, ¾ cup of sugar, the honey, brandy, lemon peel, lemon juice, and kosher salt. Set aside for 1 hour so the sugar can start to draw out the fig juices and dissolve.

2. Prepare a hot water bath (see page 30). Place the jars in it to keep warm. Wash the lids and rings in hot, soapy water, and set aside.

3. Remove the lemon peel from the pot and place the pot over medium heat. Bring to a simmer, stirring frequently. Reduce the heat to low. Simmer for about 1 hour, stirring frequently, or until the jam is thick and reduced.

4. With a handheld blender or potato masher, purée the figs. Return the mixture to a simmer.

5. Whisk together the pectin and the remaining ¼ cup of sugar. Whisk this into the jam until there are no lumps. Boil the jam for 1 minute more.

6. Ladle the jam into the prepared jars, leaving ¼ inch of headspace. Use a nonmetallic utensil to release any air bubbles. Wipe the rims clean and seal with the lids and rings.

7. Process the jars in a hot water bath (see page 31) for 10 minutes. Turn off the heat and let the jars rest in the water bath for 10 minutes.

8. Carefully remove the jars from the hot water canner. Set aside to cool for 12 hours.

9. Check the lids for proper seals (see page 32). Remove the rings, wipe the jars, label and date them, and transfer to a cupboard or pantry.

10. Refrigerate any jars that don't seal properly, and use within 6 weeks. Properly sealed jars will last in the cupboard for 12 months. Once opened, refrigerate and consume within 6 weeks.

ROSEHIP JAM

MAKES 3 QUARTER-PINT JARS

WATER-BATH CANNING, SEASONAL

Rich in vitamin C, rosehip jam is love in a jar plus immune-boosting benefits. Harvest rosehips when they are ripe and red, yet still firm. Wear gloves to prevent thorn injuries and make the process more enjoyable. While this jam is more labor intensive than others, it is well worth the work for the magnificent flavor of the finished product.

PREP TIME: 30 minutes, plus 3 days resting time
COOK TIME: 20 minutes
PROCESSING TIME: 10 minutes
TOTAL TIME: 3 days plus 1 hour

½ pound rosehips
2 cups red wine
¾ cup water
1½ cups sugar

DAYS 1 TO 3

1. Rinse the rosehips well. Cut the dark spot off the end of each and halve them. Remove the inner seeds and hairs using a small, sturdy spoon.

2. In a large bowl, cover the rosehips with the wine. Refrigerate, covered, for 3 days.

DAY 4

1. Prepare a hot water bath (see page 30). Place the jars in it to keep warm. Wash the lids and rings in hot, soapy water, and set aside.

2. Strain the rosehips.

3. In a small saucepan set over medium-high heat, combine the water and strained rosehips. Cover the pan and bring to a boil. Cook for about 10 minutes, or until the rosehips are tender.

4. Run the rosehips and their cooking water through the fine screen of a food mill.

5. Measure and return the pulp to the saucepan. There should be about 1½ cups of pulp.

6. Add the sugar, adjusting the amount, as needed, to equal the pulp amount.

Continued

ROSEHIP JAM

CONTINUED

7. Over medium-high heat, bring the jam to a full, rolling boil. Turn off the heat. Skim off any foam.

8. Ladle the jam into the prepared jars, leaving ¼ inch of headspace. Use a nonmetallic utensil to remove any air bubbles. Wipe the rims clean and seal with the lids and rings.

9. Process the jars in a hot water bath (see page 31) for 10 minutes. Turn off the heat and let the jars rest in the water bath for 10 minutes.

10. Carefully remove the jars from the hot water canner. Set aside to cool for 12 hours.

11. Check the lids for proper seals (see page 32). Remove the rings, wipe the jars, label and date them, and transfer to a cupboard or pantry.

12. Refrigerate any jars that don't seal properly, and use within 3 weeks. Properly sealed jars will last in the cupboard for 12 months. Once opened, refrigerate and consume within 3 weeks.

PREPARATION TIP

Many recipes call for waiting until after the first frost, or even several frosts, to gather rosehips. However, by this time, many of the rosehips have rotted and are unusable. It is also more difficult to remove the hairs and seeds when they are so soft. Instead, pick them as they ripen, seed them, and freeze the rosehips until you have a batch large enough to make this jam.

BLUEBERRY-ORANGE JAM

MAKES 6 HALF-PINT JARS

WATER-BATH CANNING

Blueberries taste great on their own but when combined with citrus flavors take on even more life. Try this simple blueberry and orange combination offering the best of both winter and summer flavors in one bite. Blueberries are ranked in the top spot for antioxidant activity compared to other fruits and vegetables, making them a healthy addition to any diet.

PREP TIME: 10 minutes, plus overnight resting time
COOK TIME: 30 minutes
PROCESSING TIME: 10 minutes
TOTAL TIME: 50 minutes, plus overnight resting time

2 pounds fresh blueberries
½ cup freshly squeezed orange juice, strained
2 teaspoons grated orange zest
1 cinnamon stick
4½ cups sugar

DAY 1

1. In a large pan set over medium heat, combine the blueberries, orange juice, orange zest, cinnamon stick, and sugar. Stir the mixture until the sugar dissolves. Raise the heat to high and bring to a boil. Boil for 10 minutes while stirring constantly. Turn off the heat.

2. Using a potato masher, gently mash the blueberries to the desired texture. Let the pan stand overnight at room temperature, covered with a clean kitchen towel.

DAY 2

1. Prepare a hot water bath (see page 30). Place the jars in it to keep warm. Wash the lids and rings in hot, soapy water, and set aside.

2. Place the pan over medium-high heat and bring the jam to a boil again. Cook for 15 to 20 minutes, or until it begins to thicken. Use a plate test (see page 32) to test for jam set. When to your liking, remove the cinnamon stick and skim off any foam.

3. Ladle the jam into the prepared jars, leaving ¼ inch of headspace. Use a nonmetallic utensil to remove any air bubbles. Wipe the rims clean and seal with the lids and rings.

4. Process the jars in a hot water bath (see page 31) for 10 minutes. Turn off the heat and let the jars rest in the water bath for 10 minutes.

Continued

BLUEBERRY-ORANGE JAM

CONTINUED

5. Carefully remove the jars from the hot water canner. Set aside to cool for 12 hours.

6. Check the lids for proper seals (see page 32). Remove the rings, wipe the jars, label and date them, and transfer to a cupboard or pantry.

7. Refrigerate any jars that don't seal properly, and use within 3 weeks. Properly sealed jars will last in the cupboard for 12 months. Once opened, refrigerate and consume within 3 weeks.

TRY INSTEAD

If you are lucky enough to have access to huckleberries, substitute them here for a similar, yet more complex, jam. The huckleberry, a close relative of the blueberry, is a bit more tart, but when paired with the citrus and cinnamon, it is a standout.

APPLE PIE JAM

MAKES 4 HALF-PINT JARS

WATER-BATH CANNING

Enjoy the taste bud–stimulating flavor of apple pie year-round with this simple, classic Americana jam. Use Golden Delicious apples for a crisp, fresh flavor, or substitute any apple you have on hand to make this quick treat. For best results, dice the apples quickly and get them into the water, cooking, to prevent excessive browning in the finished jam.

PREP TIME: 20 minutes
COOK TIME: 15 minutes
PROCESSING TIME: 10 minutes
TOTAL TIME: 45 minutes

2⅔ cups peeled, diced apples
½ cup water
3 tablespoons powdered pectin
3⅓ cups sugar
¾ teaspoon ground cinnamon
½ teaspoon ground nutmeg

1. Prepare a hot water bath (see page 30). Place the jars in it to keep warm. Wash the lids and rings in hot, soapy water, and set aside.

2. In a medium, covered nonreactive pot set over medium heat, combine the apples and water. Bring to a simmer and cook for about 10 minutes, or until tender.

3. Stir in the pectin. Bring the mixture to a full, rolling boil over high heat, stirring to prevent scorching.

4. Add the sugar at once and stir to combine. Bring the jam back to a rolling boil. Once it starts boiling, set a timer for 1 minute. When complete, turn off the heat and add the cinnamon and nutmeg.

5. Continue stirring the jam for about 1 minute to evenly disperse the fruit. Skim off any foam.

6. Ladle the jam into the prepared jars, leaving ¼ inch of headspace. Use a nonmetallic utensil to remove any air bubbles. Wipe the rims clean and seal with the lids and rings.

7. Process the jars in a hot water bath (see page 31) for 10 minutes. Turn off the heat and let the jars rest in the water bath for 10 minutes.

Continued

APPLE PIE JAM

CONTINUED

8. Carefully remove the jars from the hot water canner. Set aside to cool for 12 hours.

9. Check the lids for proper seals (see page 32). Remove the rings, wipe the jars, label and date them, and transfer to a cupboard or pantry.

10. Refrigerate any jars that don't seal properly, and use within 3 weeks. Properly sealed jars will last in the cupboard for 12 months. Once opened, refrigerate and consume within 3 weeks.

PREPARATION TIP

When making jam using powdered or liquid pectin, it is important to add the sugar to the fruit in one batch and not as it is measured. This can affect the set of the jam. To do this, premeasure all the sugar you need and set it aside in a bowl before the jam comes to a boil.

PLUM-ANISE JAM

MAKES 4 HALF-PINT JARS

WATER-BATH CANNING, SEASONAL

This jam works best with Italian plums, which are less juicy than many other varieties. Find them at produce markets and some specialty grocers at the height of summer when they are at their peak. They are easiest to work with (and have more natural pectin) when they are relatively firm, so there is no need to select super-ripe plums. If you can't find Italian plums, other types may be used, although an increased cooking time may be needed to achieve a nice gel.

PREP TIME: 30 minutes, plus 3 hours resting time
COOK TIME: 10 minutes
PROCESSING TIME: 10 minutes
TOTAL TIME: 3 hours, 50 minutes

5 cups chopped plums
1 ½ cups sugar
5 star anise pods
1 tablespoon freshly squeezed lemon juice

1. In a large bowl, combine the plums, sugar, and star anise. Let stand on the counter for 3 hours, covered with a clean kitchen towel.

2. Prepare a hot water bath (see page 30). Place the jars in it to keep warm. Wash the lids and rings in hot, soapy water, and set aside.

3. Remove the star anise from the jam and transfer to a nonreactive pot. Add the lemon juice. Bring to a boil. Cook for about 10 minutes and do a plate test (see page 32) to confirm set. Skim off any foam.

4. Ladle the jam into the prepared jars, leaving ¼ inch of headspace. Use a nonmetallic utensil to remove any air bubbles. Wipe the rims clean and seal with the lids and rings.

5. Process the jars in a hot water bath (see page 31) for 10 minutes. Turn off the heat and let the jars rest in the water bath for 10 minutes.

6. Carefully remove the jars from the hot water canner. Set aside to cool for 12 hours.

7. Check the lids for proper seals (see page 32). Remove the rings, wipe the jars, label and date them, and transfer to a cupboard or pantry.

8. Refrigerate any jars that don't seal properly, and use within 3 weeks. Properly sealed jars will last in the cupboard for 12 months. Once opened, refrigerate and consume within 3 weeks.

GRAPE JELLY

MAKES 4 HALF-PINT JARS

WATER-BATH CANNING, SEASONAL

Sometimes grape jelly will form harmless, tasteless crystals called tartrate crystals. To avoid them, allow the grape juice to rest overnight and then strain it through a jelly bag or a triple layer of cheesecloth before adding the pectin.

PREP TIME: 10 minutes
COOK TIME: 15 minutes, plus 8 hours chilling time
PROCESSING TIME: 5 minutes
TOTAL TIME: 8 hours, 30 minutes

2 pounds Concord grapes, stemmed
3 tablespoons liquid regular pectin
5½ cups sugar

1. In a deep pot, add the grapes and enough water to just barely cover. Crush the grapes with clean hands or a potato masher.

2. Bring to a simmer over medium-high heat. Reduce the heat to low and continue to cook for about 10 minutes, or until the grapes have burst and the juices are released.

3. In a wire sieve set over a bowl, strain the grapes. Use a spoon or spatula to push the seeds and skin out of the way to help the juices drain. Discard the seeds, skin, and pulp. Chill the juice in the refrigerator for 8 hours.

4. Suspend a jelly bag over a bowl or line a colander with a triple layer of rinsed cheesecloth. Pour in the grape juice. Let it drain, without pressing or squeezing. Measure 4 cups of juice. Use the remainder, if any, to make a second batch.

5. Prepare a hot water bath (see page 30). Place the jars in it to keep warm. Wash the lids and rings in hot, soapy water, and set aside.

6. In a preserving pot or deep pot, combine the grape juice and the pectin. Bring to a rolling boil over high heat. Add the sugar and stir well to dissolve. Return to a full boil for 1 minute.

7. Ladle the jelly into the prepared jars, leaving ¼ inch of headspace. Use a nonmetallic utensil to release any air bubbles. Wipe the rims clean and seal with the lids and rings.

8. Process the jars in a hot water bath (see page 31) for 5 minutes, then turn off the heat and let the jars rest in the water bath for 10 minutes.

9. Carefully remove the jars from the hot water canner. Set aside to cool for 12 hours.

10. Check the lids for proper seals (see page 32). Remove the rings, wipe the jars, label and date them, and then transfer to a cupboard or pantry.

11. Refrigerate any jars that don't seal properly, and use within 3 weeks. Properly sealed jars will last in the cupboard for 12 months. Once opened, refrigerate and consume within 3 weeks.

POMEGRANATE JELLY

MAKES 6 HALF-PINT JARS

WATER-BATH CANNING

Serve this ruby-red jelly instead of the traditional cranberry jelly the next time you roast a turkey, or stir a spoonful into a cup of hot tea. If you don't want the bother of making your own pomegranate juice, you can find bottled juice in many stores. Check the label to be sure it is pure pomegranate juice, not a juice blend or cocktail.

PREP TIME: 15 minutes, plus 3 hours draining time
COOK TIME: 5 minutes
PROCESSING TIME: 5 minutes
TOTAL TIME: 3 hours, 25 minutes

2 whole pomegranates
2½ cups dry red wine, such as merlot, zinfandel, malbec, or amarone)
6 tablespoons liquid pectin
4½ cups sugar
½ cup freshly squeezed lemon juice

1. Cut the pomegranates in half through the middle. Working over a colander set in a bowl, break apart the pomegranate and scoop out the pockets of seeds with your fingers or a spoon. Discard the rinds and any of the white membrane connecting the seeds.

2. With clean hands or a potato masher, crush the pomegranate seeds and let the juice drain. If you press on the seeds, you may extract more juice but the jelly may not be perfectly clear.

3. Suspend a jelly bag over a bowl or line a colander with a triple layer of rinsed cheesecloth and pour in the pomegranate juice. Let it drain for 2 to 3 hours without pressing or squeezing. Measure 1 cup of juice. Use the remainder, if any, to make a second batch or to drink.

4. Prepare a hot water bath (see page 30). Place the jars in it to keep warm. Wash the lids and rings in hot, soapy water, and set aside.

5. In a preserving pot or deep pot set over high heat, combine the pomegranate juice, wine, and pectin. Bring to a rolling boil.

6. Add the sugar and lemon juice. Stir well to dissolve. Return to a full boil for 1 minute.

7. Ladle the hot jelly into the prepared jars, leaving ¼ inch of headspace. Use a nonmetallic utensil to release any air bubbles. Wipe the rims clean and seal with the lids and rings.

Continued

POMEGRANATE JELLY

CONTINUED

8. Process the jars in a hot water bath (see page 31) for 5 minutes. Turn off the heat and let the jars rest in the water bath for 10 minutes.

9. Carefully remove the jars from the hot water canner. Set aside to cool for 12 hours.

10. Check the lids for proper seals (see page 32). Remove the rings, wipe the jars, label and date them, and transfer to a cupboard or pantry.

11. Refrigerate any jars that don't seal properly, and use within 3 weeks. Properly sealed jars will last in the cupboard for 12 months. Once opened, refrigerate and consume within 3 weeks.

A CLOSER LOOK

One pomegranate has about 600 seeds and produces about ½ cup of juice. If you don't want to stain your fingers, put a halved pomegranate in a big bowl of water and work out the seeds under water. The bits of membrane will rise to the surface so they are easy to remove.

SPICED ELDERBERRY JELLY

MAKES 4 HALF-PINT JARS

WATER-BATH CANNING, SEASONAL

Elderberry, a seasonal treat available from early to late summer, depending on your location, is similar in flavor to a blackberry or blueberry. While great in jam, *elderberries should not be eaten raw*—so resist snacking while you prepare this jam. Notable for their use in alternative medicine, elderberries are thought to have anti-viral and anti-inflammatory properties.

PREP TIME: 20 minutes, plus overnight draining time
COOK TIME: 1 hour, 40 minutes
PROCESSING TIME: 5 minutes
TOTAL TIME: 2 hours, 5 minutes plus overnight draining time

1 pound fresh elderberries
1 pound apples, cored and roughly chopped
Zest of 1 small mandarin-type orange
1 cinnamon stick
1 star anise pod
2 cloves
2 allspice berries
2½ cups sugar

DAY 1

1. In the sink, rinse the elderberries well.

2. Working over a large bowl to catch the berries and their juices, remove the berries from their stems using the tines of a fork.

3. In a large saucepan set over low heat, combine the berries and apples. Cover with water. Simmer for about 1 hour, or until very soft.

4. Set a large bowl below a jelly bag. Pour the fruit and juice into the bag and allow the mixture to drip overnight.

DAY 2

1. Prepare a hot water bath (see page 30). Place the jars in it to keep warm. Wash the lids and rings in hot, soapy water, and set aside.

2. In a cheesecloth square, combine the orange zest, cinnamon stick, star anise, cloves, and allspice berries. Tie securely with kitchen twine into a sachet.

3. In a medium saucepan, combine 2½ cups of elderberry juice, the sachet, and the sugar. Bring to a full, rolling boil. Cook for 30 to 40 minutes, or until it thickens, or reaches 220°F, measured with a candy thermometer. Stir regularly to prevent scorching.

Continued

SPICED ELDERBERRY JELLY

CONTINUED

4. Once the jelly reaches 220°F and maintains this temperature for 1 minute, turn off the heat. Use the plate test to determine set (see page 32). If not, return the pot to the burner and cook in 5-minute increments until it sets to your liking. Turn off the heat, remove the sachet, and skim off any foam.

5. Ladle the jelly into the prepared jars, leaving ¼ inch of headspace. Use a nonmetallic utensil to release any air bubbles. Wipe the rims clean and seal with the lids and rings.

6. Process the jars in a hot water bath (see page 31) for 5 minutes. Turn off the heat and let the jars rest in the water bath for 10 minutes.

7. Carefully remove the jars from the hot water canner. Set aside to cool for 12 hours.

8. Check the lids for proper seals (see page 32). Remove the rings, wipe the jars, label and date them, and transfer to a cupboard or pantry.

9. Refrigerate any jars that don't seal properly, and use within 3 weeks. Properly sealed jars will last in the cupboard for 12 months. Once opened, refrigerate and consume within 3 weeks.

HOT PEPPER–CRABAPPLE JELLY

MAKES 6 HALF-PINT JARS

WATER-BATH CANNING

Crabapples are a type of wild apple found throughout North America. They have a beautiful pink color when preserved. Crabapples are small, usually less than 2 inches in diameter, with an incredibly sour taste. That's why they are most often made into preserves—to tame their tartness with sugar. The acid in the crabapples compensates for the lack of acid in the peppers and their pectin helps the fruit gel without added pectin.

PREP TIME: 20 minutes
COOK TIME: 40 minutes, plus 1 hour draining time
PROCESSING TIME: 5 minutes
TOTAL TIME: 2 hours, 5 minutes

- 2 pounds crabapples, stemmed and coarsely chopped
- 1 ½ cups water
- ½ cup red wine vinegar, as needed
- 3¾ cups granulated sugar
- 1 cup chopped green bell pepper
- ⅓ cup chopped chile peppers, green, red hot, or a combination (jalapeños, serranos, ancho, Fresno, Scotch bonnet, etc.)

1. In a deep pot set over high heat, combine the crabapples and water. Bring to a boil. Reduce the heat to low. Simmer for 20 to 25 minutes, or until tender.

2. Suspend a jelly bag over a bowl, or line a colander with a triple layer of rinsed cheesecloth, and pour in the crabapples. Let them drain for 1 hour, without pressing or squeezing. Measure the juice and add enough red wine vinegar to make 3 cups.

3. Prepare a hot water bath (see page 30). Place the jars in it to keep warm. Wash the lids and rings in hot, soapy water, and set aside.

4. In a large saucepan set over high heat, combine the crabapple juice mixture and sugar. Bring to a rolling boil.

5. Add the green bell pepper and chile peppers. Continue to boil for 5 to 10 minutes, or until the jelly is set and the mixture reaches 220°F, measured with a candy thermometer. Test for gel after 5 minutes (see page 32).

6. Turn off the heat. Continue stirring frequently for another 5 to 6 minutes.

7. Ladle the hot jelly into the prepared jars, leaving ¼ inch of headspace. Use a nonmetallic utensil to release any air bubbles. Wipe the rims clean and seal with the lids and rings.

Continued

HOT PEPPER-CRABAPPLE JELLY

CONTINUED

8. Process the jars in a hot water bath (see page 31) for 5 minutes. Turn off the heat and let the jars rest in the water bath for 10 minutes.

9. Carefully remove the jars from the hot water canner. Set aside to cool for 12 hours.

10. Check the lids for proper seals (see page 32). Remove the rings, wipe the jars, label and date them, and transfer to a cupboard or pantry.

11. Refrigerate any jars that don't seal properly, and use within 3 weeks. Properly sealed jars will last in the cupboard for 12 months. Once opened, refrigerate and consume within 3 weeks.

PAIR IT

A classic presentation for this jelly is spread over a room-temperature block of cream cheese and served with plenty of crackers. Try it on turkey or chicken sandwiches, too.

CLASSIC ORANGE MARMALADE

MAKES 5 HALF-PINT JARS

WATER-BATH CANNING

This marmalade is made with navel oranges, along with a few lemons to counter the orange's natural sweetness. The rind adds the bitter flavor. Look for organic fruits. Conventional produce is sprayed with insecticides, which can gather in the rind. Keep track of how much water you add when simmering the citrus fruits. You will need to add extra sugar, equal to the amount of added water, to get a nicely set marmalade.

PREP TIME: 20 minutes
COOK TIME: 2 hours
PROCESSING TIME: 5 minutes
TOTAL TIME: 2 hours, 25 minutes

2 pounds navel oranges
3 lemons
4 cups water, plus additional as needed
4 cups sugar, plus additional as needed
Pinch salt
2 tablespoons Scotch (optional)

1. Cut the blossom end (with the dimple) from the oranges and lemons. Slice the fruit as thinly as possible, less than ¼ inch thick. Remove the seeds, stack the slices, and cut into quarters.

2. In a preserving pot or a deep pot set over high heat, add the oranges and lemons. Add the water, plus additional if needed, to just barely cover the fruit. Bring to a boil. Reduce the heat to medium. Simmer for 45 minutes to 1 hour, or until very tender.

3. Prepare a hot water bath (see page 30). Place the jars in it to keep warm. Wash the lids and rings in hot, soapy water, and set aside.

4. Add the sugar to the pot of fruit, plus any additional sugar needed to equal any additional water added. Bring to a simmer over medium-low heat. Add the salt and Scotch (if using). Simmer for 45 minutes to 1 hour, stirring frequently, or until the marmalade gels and the mixture reaches 220°F, measured with a candy thermometer. Test for gel after 45 minutes (see page 32).

5. Ladle the marmalade into the prepared jars, leaving ½ inch of headspace. Use a nonmetallic utensil to release any air bubbles. Wipe the rims clean and seal with the lids and rings.

6. Process the jars in a hot water bath (see page 31) for 5 minutes. Turn off the heat and let the jars rest in the water bath for 10 minutes.

Continued

CLASSIC ORANGE MARMALADE

CONTINUED

7. Carefully remove the jars from the hot water canner. Set aside to cool for 12 hours.

8. Check the lids for proper seals (see page 32). Remove the rings, wipe the jars, label and date them, and transfer to a cupboard or pantry.

9. Refrigerate any jars that don't seal properly, and use within 3 weeks. Properly sealed jars will last in the cupboard for 12 months. Once opened, refrigerate and consume within 3 weeks.

TRY INSTEAD

Sour, or Seville, oranges are sometimes available midwinter. Their bitter, sweet, and delicious orange flavor can be substituted for the lemons in this recipe. To make a grapefruit marmalade, substitute pink or red grapefruits for the navel oranges, or choose a variety of citrus fruits, including lemons, limes, grapefruit, and pomelo, as long as the combined weight of the citrus is about 3 pounds.

STRAWBERRY, BLACKBERRY, LEMON MARMALADE

MAKES 4 HALF-PINT JARS

WATER-BATH CANNING

Strawberries and blackberries pair with lemon to create this bright fruit marmalade that tastes like summer in a jar. Using pectin to ensure a fast and foolproof set, this quick marmalade is a spectacular seasonal treat. It requires little time by the stove during the heat of summer when strawberries and blackberries are at their peak.

PREP TIME: 15 minutes
COOK TIME: 5 minutes
PROCESSING TIME: 10 minutes
TOTAL TIME: 30 minutes

- 1 lemon
- 1 ¾ cups fresh strawberries, hulled and crushed
- 1 cup fresh blackberries, crushed
- 1 ½ teaspoons freshly squeezed lemon juice
- 3 tablespoons powdered pectin
- 3 ½ cups sugar

1. Prepare a hot water bath (see page 30). Place the jars in it to keep warm. Wash the lids and rings in hot, soapy water, and set aside.

2. Wash the lemon well with warm, soapy water. With a sharp knife, cut away half of the rind from the lemon, removing as much of the pith (white inner membrane) as possible. Slice the rind into thin strips, and then cut the strips into ¼-inch-long pieces.

3. In a small saucepot set over high heat, combine the lemon rind with enough water to cover. Bring to a boil. Strain and reserve the rind.

4. In a medium saucepot set over high heat, combine the strawberries, blackberries, lemon rind, and lemon juice. Slowly stir in the pectin. Bring the mixture to a full, rolling boil.

5. Add the sugar. Return the mixture to a full, rolling boiling over high heat. When the jam cannot be stirred down, set a timer for 1 minute and stir constantly. Turn off the heat.

6. With the heat off, stir the marmalade for 1 minute more to ensure even distribution of the rind before filling the jars. Skim off any foam.

7. Ladle the marmalade into the prepared jars, leaving ¼ inch of headspace. Use a nonmetallic utensil to remove any air bubbles. Wipe the rims clean and seal with the lids and rings.

Continued

STRAWBERRY, BLACKBERRY, LEMON MARMALADE

CONTINUED

8. Process the jars in a hot water bath (see page 31) for 10 minutes. Turn off the heat and let the jars rest in the water bath for 10 minutes.

9. Carefully remove the jars from the hot water canner. Set aside to cool for 12 hours.

10. Check the lids for proper seals (see page 32). Remove the rings, wipe the jars, label and date them, and transfer to a cupboard or pantry.

11. Refrigerate any jars that don't seal properly, and use within 3 weeks. Properly sealed jars will last in the cupboard for 12 months. Once opened, refrigerate and consume within 3 weeks.

LOW-SUGAR PREPARATION TIP

This recipe can be converted to a reduced-sugar recipe simply by scaling back on the amount of sugar used. Using a standard powder pectin, the amount of sugar can be reduced to 2 cups and still achieve a good set. Don't reduce the amount of sugar any more than this, however, as you may get a jam that does not set.

GRAPEFRUIT-VANILLA MARMALADE

MAKES 4 HALF-PINT JARS

WATER-BATH CANNING

Grapefruit is best in the winter when its natural sweetness shines brightest. Using ruby red grapefruit produces the most flavorful, fruity, and vibrantly colored marmalade. Other varieties can also create a delicious, though less colorful, marmalade. Blanching the grapefruit peel reduces bitterness and allows for its inclusion for that traditional marmalade texture.

PREP TIME: 25 minutes
COOK TIME: 1 hour, 10 minutes
PROCESSING TIME: 10 minutes
TOTAL TIME: 1 hour, 45 minutes

3 grapefruits
3 cups sugar
1 whole vanilla bean, split lengthwise, seeds scraped out and reserved

1. Prepare a hot water bath (see page 30). Place the jars in it to keep warm. Wash the lids and rings in hot, soapy water, and set aside.

2. Wash the grapefruits well with warm, soapy water. With a sharp knife, remove the grapefruit rind. Stack into piles and slice into strips. Mince the strips.

3. In a small saucepan over medium heat, combine the minced rind with enough water to cover. Bring to a simmer. Cook for 20 minutes, or until tender.

4. While the rind cooks, remove any remaining pith from the grapefruit with your hands or a knife. Working over a bowl to catch the juice, slice along the membranes, removing each grapefruit segment individually. Add the segments to the bowl with the juice. When finished, squeeze the remaining membranes over the bowl to collect any additional juice. Discard the membranes and seeds.

5. Strain the rind, reserving 2 cups of the cooking liquid.

6. In a medium saucepot set over medium-high heat, combine the reserved cooking liquid, sugar, rind, and the grapefruit segments in their juices. Bring to a full, rolling boil. Cook for 30 to 45 minutes, or until it reaches 220°F, measured with a candy thermometer.

Continued

GRAPEFRUIT-VANILLA MARMALADE

CONTINUED

7. Add the vanilla bean seeds. Turn off the heat. Use the plate test to determine if the marmalade sets (see page 32). If not, return the pot to the burner and cook in 5-minute increments until it sets to your liking.

8. With the heat off, stir the marmalade for 1 minute to evenly distribute the rind. Skim off any foam.

9. Ladle the marmalade into the prepared jars, leaving ¼ inch of headspace. Use a nonmetallic utensil to remove any air bubbles. Wipe the rims clean and seal using the lids and rings.

10. Process the jars in a hot water bath (see page 31) for 10 minutes. Turn off the heat and let the jars rest in the water bath for 10 minutes.

11. Carefully remove the jars from the hot water canner. Set aside to cool for 12 hours.

12. Check the lids for proper seals (see page 32). Remove the rings, wipe the jars, label and date them, and transfer to a cupboard or pantry.

13. Refrigerate any jars that don't seal properly, and use within 3 weeks. Properly sealed jars will last in the cupboard for 12 months. Once opened, refrigerate and consume within 3 weeks.

DID YOU KNOW?

The grapefruit is a cross between an orange and a pomelo. First found in Barbados in the eighteenth century, the fruit developed naturally. It took some time to gain popularity, perhaps because of its bitterness and difficulty to peel. In the twentieth century, the grapefruit underwent a natural change. Red grapefruits developed from seedlings. Today, most of the cultivated grapefruits are the red variety, which are grown in Florida, Arizona, Texas, and California.

WILD STRAWBERRY PRESERVES

MAKES 3 PINT JARS, OR 6 HALF-PINT JARS

WATER-BATH CANNING, SEASONAL

The four-day process for making these preserves is meant to keep the berries as plump and bright red as possible. Instead of simply cooking the berries with sugar—which can leave them limp and pale—only the juices are cooked on the first two days. This gives the berries plenty of time to plump up on sugar before being cooked with syrup and jarred.

PREP TIME: 15 minutes, plus 3 days' resting time
COOK TIME: 30 minutes
PROCESSING TIME: 10 minutes
TOTAL TIME: 55 minutes, plus 3 days' resting time

1 quart fresh wild strawberries, hulled
2 cups sugar, plus additional as needed

DAY 1

1. In a large bowl, combine the strawberries and the sugar. Toss gently to coat evenly.

2. Cover and rest overnight at room temperature.

DAY 2

1. With a sieve set over a medium saucepan to catch the syrup, strain the berries. Return the strained berries to the bowl.

2. Bring the syrup to a boil over high heat. Taste, and add more sugar if too tart. Cool to room temperature. Pour the liquid over the berries. Cover and rest overnight again at room temperature.

DAY 3

Repeat Steps 1 and 2 from Day 2—draining the berries, reducing the syrup, and letting them rest overnight again.

Continued

WILD STRAWBERRY PRESERVES

CONTINUED

DAY 4

1. Prepare a hot water bath (see page 30). Place the jars in it to keep warm. Wash the lids and rings in hot, soapy water, and set aside.

2. Drain the strawberries as before, catching the syrup in a pan. Set the drained berries aside.

3. Bring the syrup to a boil over high heat. Add the strawberries. Reduce the heat to low. Simmer for about 20 minutes, until the syrup is reduced by one-fourth, or reduced and beginning to thicken. There will be a noticeable gelling at this point.

4. Ladle the hot strawberry preserves into the prepared jars, leaving ¼ inch of headspace. Use a nonmetallic utensil to release any air bubbles. Wipe the rims clean and seal with the lids and rings.

5. Process the jars in a hot water bath (see page 31) for 10 minutes. Turn off the heat and let the jars rest in the water bath for 10 minutes.

6. Carefully remove the jars from the hot water canner. Set aside to cool for 12 hours.

7. Check the lids for proper seals (see page 32). Remove the rings, wipe the jars, label and date them, and transfer to a cupboard or pantry.

8. Refrigerate any jars that don't seal properly, and use within 3 weeks. Properly sealed jars will last in the cupboard for 12 months. Once opened, refrigerate and consume within 3 weeks.

APRICOT PRESERVES

MAKES 3 PINT JARS, OR 6 HALF-PINT JARS

WATER-BATH CANNING

Some recipes for apricot preserves may call for adding some of the apricot kernels, tied in a sachet, while the preserves simmer. This adds an unusual, almond-like essence to the preserves. Add only two or three kernels to a batch this size as they contain a substance that can be toxic above a certain level. If you'd like the flavor without having to crack open the apricot pits, simply add a drop or two of almond extract during the last few minutes of cooking time.

PREP TIME: 15 minutes
COOK TIME: 1 hour, 10 minutes
PROCESSING TIME: 10 minutes
TOTAL TIME: 1 hour, 35 minutes

1⅓ cups sugar
¼ cup water
2½ pounds fresh apricots, pitted, divided
2 tablespoons freshly squeezed lemon juice

1. Prepare a hot water bath (see page 30). Place the jars in it to keep warm. Wash the lids and rings in hot, soapy water, and set aside.

2. In a small saucepan set over medium heat, combine the sugar and water. Stir for about 4 minutes, or until the sugar is completely dissolved and has a thick, syrupy consistency.

3. Add half of the apricots to the sugar syrup. Simmer for about 30 minutes, or until the fruit is almost falling apart. Add the remaining half of the apricots. Continue simmering for another 30 minutes, or until almost tender enough to fall apart, but still holding their shape.

4. Stir in the lemon juice. Simmer an additional 5 minutes.

5. Ladle the hot apricot preserves into the prepared jars, leaving ¼ inch of headspace. Use a nonmetallic utensil to release any air bubbles. Wipe the rims clean and seal with the lids and rings.

6. Process the jars in a hot water bath (see page 31) for 10 minutes. Turn off the heat and let the jars rest in the water bath for 10 minutes.

Continued

APRICOT PRESERVES

CONTINUED

7. Carefully remove the jars from the hot water canner. Set aside to cool for 12 hours.

8. Check the lids for proper seals (see page 32). Remove the rings, wipe the jars, label and date them, and transfer to a cupboard or pantry.

9. Refrigerate any jars that don't seal properly, and use within 3 weeks. Properly sealed jars will last in the cupboard for 12 months. Once opened, refrigerate and consume within 3 weeks.

PREPARATION TIP:

To prepare apricot kernels for a sachet, use a nutcracker or hammer to break open two or three apricot pits. Pry out the kernels and tie them in cheesecloth. Add this sachet during the last 30 minutes of simmering. Remember to remove and discard it before putting the preserves into jars.

CHERRY TOMATO PRESERVES

MAKES 8 HALF-PINT JARS, OR 4 PINT JARS

WATER-BATH CANNING

If you've struck gold with over-producing cherry tomato plants, make the most of your luck. Make extra preserves—a sweet and tart tomato jam—to savor this winter or give as gifts. You'll find plenty of occasions to enjoy these tomatoes. They're perfect for serving on toasted or grilled breads as classic antipasti or simply spooned over fresh ricotta and topped with a few slivers of fresh basil.

PREP TIME: 20 minutes
COOK TIME: 45 minutes
PROCESSING TIME: 15 minutes for half-pint jars; 20 minutes for pint jars
TOTAL TIME: 1 hour, 20 to 25 minutes

3 tablespoons extra-virgin olive oil
2 pounds yellow onions, cut into ½-inch-thick slices
4 cups halved cherry tomatoes
¾ cup honey
1 fresh wild fennel stalk, chopped, or 1 teaspoon fennel seed, tied in a cheesecloth sachet
Balsamic vinegar, for seasoning
Freshly ground black pepper, for seasoning
Kosher salt, for seasoning
4 teaspoons citric acid, divided

1. Prepare a hot water bath (see page 30). Place the jars in it to keep warm. Wash the lids and rings in hot, soapy water, and set aside.

2. In a preserving pot or a large saucepan set over medium heat, add the olive oil to heat.

3. Add the onions. Cook for about 35 minutes, stirring frequently, or until very tender and golden-brown.

4. Stir in the tomatoes and honey. Bring to a simmer.

5. Add the fennel stalk. Simmer for about 10 minutes, or until the mixture thickens. It should hold its shape slightly when dropped from a spoon.

6. Season with the balsamic vinegar, pepper, and kosher salt.

Continued

CHERRY TOMATO PRESERVES

CONTINUED

7. Spoon citric acid into each jar: ½ teaspoon per half-pint jar or 1 teaspoon per pint jar.

8. Ladle the hot preserves into the prepared jars, leaving ½ inch of headspace. Use a nonmetallic utensil to release any air bubbles. Wipe the rims clean and seal with the lids and rings.

9. Process the jars in a hot water bath (see page 31): half-pint jars for 15 minutes, or pint jars for 20 minutes. Turn off the heat and let the jars rest in the water bath for 10 minutes.

10. Carefully remove the jars from the hot water canner. Set aside to cool for 12 hours.

11. Check the lids for proper seals (see page 32). Remove the rings, wipe the jars, label and date them, and transfer the jars to a cupboard or pantry.

12. Refrigerate any jars that don't seal properly, and use within 2 months. Properly sealed jars will last in the cupboard for 12 months. Once opened, refrigerate and consume within 2 months.

HONEYED FIGS WITH WILD FENNEL

MAKES 5 HALF-PINT JARS

WATER-BATH CANNING, SEASONAL

Honeyed figs are a type of spoon sweet—easily enjoyed directly from the spoon—traditionally served to guests along with mint tea throughout Eastern Europe and North Africa. This recipe calls for two specific ingredients you might not easily find: wild fennel seed and sage honey. Wild fennel has a light, captivating aroma with a hint of licorice. It is typically sold as dried powder, pollen, and seeds. Sage honey is produced from bees that feed on sage blossoms, giving the preserves a sweet, herbal quality. Both add a subtlety that is worth the effort to find them, but using good, locally produced honey and regular fennel seed will also produce a great product.

PREP TIME: 10 minutes, plus overnight resting time
COOK TIME: 15 minutes
PROCESSING TIME: 10 minutes
TOTAL TIME: 35 minutes, plus overnight resting time

2¼ pounds Black Mission or brown Turkish figs, ends trimmed and halved (6 cups)
4 cups sugar
½ cup sage honey
Juice of 1 lemon
3 California bay leaves
½ teaspoon wild fennel seed
Zest of 1 lemon (optional)

DAY 1

In a large container, toss together the figs, sugar, honey, lemon juice, bay leaves, and fennel seed. Cover and refrigerate overnight.

DAY 2

1. Prepare a hot water bath (see page 30). Place the jars in it to keep warm. Wash the lids and rings in hot, soapy water, and set aside.

2. In a preserving pot or a large saucepot set over high heat, add the figs and any accumulated juices. Bring to a full rolling boil, stirring frequently. Reduce the heat to low. Simmer for about 10 minutes, or until the liquid reduces and the preserves are quite thick.

Continued

HONEYED FIGS WITH WILD FENNEL

CONTINUED

3. Stir in the lemon zest (if using). Simmer for 2 minutes more.

4. Ladle the preserves into the prepared jars, leaving ¼ inch of headspace. Use a nonmetallic utensil to release any air bubbles. Wipe the rims clean and seal with the lids and rings.

5. Process the jars in a hot water bath (see page 31) for 10 minutes. Turn off the heat and let the jars rest in the water bath for 10 minutes.

6. Carefully remove the jars from the hot water canner. Set aside to cool for 12 hours.

7. Check the lids for proper seals (see page 32). Remove the rings, wipe the jars, label and date them, and transfer to a cupboard or pantry.

8. Refrigerate any jars that don't seal properly, and use within 3 weeks. Properly sealed jars will last in the cupboard for 12 months. Once opened, refrigerate and consume within 3 weeks.

KUMQUATS IN SYRUP

MAKES 3 HALF-PINT JARS

WATER-BATH CANNING

Kumquats are available around the same time as pomegranates, making them a popular addition to holiday wreaths and centerpieces. If you like the tart and bitter taste of kumquats, this preserve is a great way to enjoy them.

PREP TIME: 5 minutes
COOK TIME: 45 minutes
PROCESSING TIME: 10 minutes
TOTAL TIME: 1 hour

4 to 5 cups whole kumquats
1 ½ cups sugar
¾ cup water, plus additional for blanching
1 cinnamon stick
2 whole cardamom pods
1 whole clove

1. Prepare a hot water bath (see page 30). Place the jars in it to keep warm. Wash the lids and rings in hot, soapy water, and set aside.

2. In a large saucepot set over high heat, combine the kumquats with enough fresh cold water to cover by 1 inch. Bring to a boil. Drain in a colander and rinse. Repeat this step two more times, using fresh water each time.

3. Return the blanched kumquats to the saucepot. Add the sugar, water, cinnamon stick, cardamom pods, and clove. Bring to a full rolling boil over high heat, stirring constantly to dissolve the sugar. Reduce the heat to low. Simmer for about 30 minutes, or until the kumquats are tender and the syrup is quite thick.

4. With a slotted spoon, transfer the kumquats, evenly divided, into the prepared jars. Ladle the syrup over, filling the jars to within ¼ inch of the rim. Use a nonmetallic utensil to release any air bubbles in the syrup. Wipe the rims clean and seal with the lids and rings.

5. Process the jars in a hot water bath (see page 31) for 10 minutes. Turn off the heat and let the jars rest in the water bath for 10 minutes.

6. Carefully remove the jars from the hot water canner. Set aside to cool for 12 hours.

7. Check the lids for proper seals (see page 32). Remove the rings, wipe the jars, label and date them, and transfer to a cupboard or pantry.

8. Refrigerate any jars that don't seal properly, and use within 3 weeks. Properly sealed jars will last in the cupboard for 12 months. Once opened, refrigerate and consume within 3 weeks.

4

CONSERVES, BUTTERS, CHEESES & CURDS

These lesser-known fruit products are packed with flavor and intrigue, and they don't need to be saved for high tea or special occasions. Simple to make and bursting with creativity, you can use these products just like jam and spread them on bread or add them to tarts and other sweet treats for an unlikely and welcome twist of flavor.

RED CURRANT AND ORANGE CONSERVE

MAKES 6 HALF-PINT JARS

WATER-BATH CANNING, SEASONAL

Fresh red currants aren't always easy to find, unless you have a bush in your yard. The berries are quite fragile. If you buy them in quantity, be prepared to process them into conserves and jelly within a day or two. Add some chopped pecans or walnuts, if you like. This conserve is a perfect match for the rich flavors of roasted or grilled pork or salmon.

PREP TIME: 5 minutes, plus overnight resting time
COOK TIME: 25 minutes
PROCESSING TIME: 10 minutes
TOTAL TIME: 40 minutes, plus overnight resting time

3 pounds fresh red currants
2½ cups sugar
½ cup freshly squeezed orange juice
Peel of 1 orange, finely sliced
Juice of 1 lemon

DAY 1

In a large container, layer the currants and sugar. Cover and refrigerate overnight.

DAY 2

1. Prepare a hot water bath (see page 30). Place the jars in it to keep warm. Wash the lids and rings in hot, soapy water, and set aside.

2. Set a large pot over medium heat. Transfer the currants and their juices to the pot. Stir in the orange juice, orange peel, and lemon juice. Bring to a full rolling boil. Cook for 20 to 25 minutes, stirring frequently, or until the conserve gels and the mixture reaches 220°F, measured with a candy thermometer. Test for gel after 20 minutes (see page 32).

3. Ladle the conserves into the prepared jars, leaving ¼ inch of headspace. Use a nonmetallic utensil to release any air bubbles. Wipe the rims clean and seal with the lids and rings.

4. Process the jars in a hot water bath (see page 31) for 10 minutes. Turn off the heat and let the jars rest in the water bath for 10 minutes.

5. Carefully remove the jars from the hot water canner. Set aside to cool for 12 hours.

6. Check the lids for proper seals (see page 32). Remove the rings, wipe the jars, label and date them, and transfer to a cupboard or pantry.

7. Refrigerate any jars that don't seal properly, and use within 3 weeks. Properly sealed jars will last in the cupboard for 12 months. Once opened, refrigerate and consume within 3 weeks.

GOLDEN SUMMER CONSERVE

MAKES 4 HALF-PINT JARS

WATER-BATH-CANNING, LOW-SUGAR

Because the sweetness of the peaches and nectarines shines, this low-sugar conserve has the full-fruit flavor of a typical conserve with just a fraction of the sugar. Use Pomona's Pectin, as no other low-sugar pectin can withstand such low levels of sugar and still set well.

PREP TIME: 30 minutes
COOK TIME: 15 minutes
PROCESSING TIME: 10 minutes
TOTAL TIME: 55 minutes

½ teaspoon of calcium powder, included with the Pomona's Pectin
1 ½ cups water, divided
1 ½ pounds peaches, peeled, pitted, and diced
1 pound nectarines, pitted and diced
½ cup golden raisins
½ cup sliced almonds
½ cup freshly squeezed lemon juice
¾ cup sugar
3 teaspoons Pomona's Pectin

1. In a small bowl, prepare the calcium water by combining the calcium powder with ½ cup of water. Set aside.

2. Prepare a hot water bath (see page 30). Place the jars in it to keep warm. Wash the lids and rings in hot, soapy water, and set aside.

3. In a large pot, combine the peaches, nectarines, golden raisins, almonds, and remaining 1 cup of water. Bring to a boil. Reduce the heat to low. Simmer for about 5 minutes, or until the fruit is uniformly soft. Turn off the heat. Stir well to mix.

4. Measure 4 cups of the fruit-almond mixture. Refrigerate any leftovers for another use. To the 4 cups of conserve, add 4 teaspoons of the calcium water and the lemon juice. Mix well to combine.

5. Pour the conserve back into the pot. Bring to a boil over medium-high heat.

6. Meanwhile, in a medium bowl, measure the sugar and pectin. Stir well to combine.

7. When a rolling boil occurs, slowly add the pectin/sugar mixture, stirring to combine. Stir continuously as the sugar dissolves. Once it returns to a boil, remove the pot from the heat.

8. Ladle the conserves into the prepared jars, leaving ¼ inch of headspace. Use a nonmetallic utensil to release any air bubbles. Wipe the rims clean and seal with the lids and rings.

Continued

GOLDEN SUMMER CONSERVE

CONTINUED

9. Process the jars in a hot water bath (see page 31) for 10 minutes. Turn off the heat and let the jars rest in the water bath for 10 minutes.

10. Carefully remove the jars from the hot water canner. Set aside to cool for 12 hours.

11. Check the lids for proper seals (see page 32). Remove the rings, wipe the jars, label and date them, and transfer to a cupboard or pantry.

12. Refrigerate any jars that don't seal properly, and use within 3 weeks. Properly sealed jars will last in the cupboard for 12 months. Once opened, refrigerate and consume within 3 weeks.

PAIR IT

Conserves taste great on bread, scones, English muffins, pancakes, or waffles. The addition of nuts means they pair wonderfully with many types of meats and cheeses, making them a flavor booster for party platters or antipasto trays. To heighten the flavor of cakes and pies, conserves can also be served alongside.

GRAPE CONSERVE

MAKES 4 HALF-PINT JARS

WATER-BATH CANNING, SEASONAL

Concord grapes come around just once a year, in the late summer and early fall. Preservers know that though these grapes require a bit of work to remove the seeds, the end flavor result is well worth the effort. Look for Concord grapes at farmers' markets toward the end of the summer, when they begin to ripen. Try this simple, no-pectin conserve that makes the most of this seasonal bounty.

PREP TIME: 20 minutes
COOK TIME: 30 minutes
PROCESSING TIME: 5 minutes
TOTAL TIME: 55 minutes

2½ cups Concord grapes, skinned, skins reserved
1 mandarin orange, or other small orange
2 cups sugar
½ cup golden raisins
¼ teaspoon salt
½ cup walnuts, chopped

1. Prepare a hot water bath (see page 30). Place the jars in it to keep warm. Wash the lids and rings in hot, soapy water, and set aside.

2. To a small pot set over high heat, add grapes. Bring to a boil. Cook for about 10 minutes, stirring constantly, or until the seeds begin to show.

3. Pass the grapes through a food mill to remove the seeds. Return the grape flesh and any juices to the pot.

4. Wash the orange well in soapy water and chop it finely without peeling. Remove any seeds.

5. To the grapes, add the orange, sugar, golden raisins, and salt. Bring the mixture to a boil over high heat, stirring constantly for about 10 minutes.

6. Add the reserved grape skins. Continue cooking for an additional 10 minutes, or until the conserve begins to thicken. Remove from the heat, stir in the walnuts, and skim off any foam. The conserve will thicken after cooling so do not overcook it.

7. Ladle the conserves into the prepared jars, leaving ¼ inch of headspace. Use a nonmetallic utensil to release any air bubbles. Wipe the rims clean and seal with the lids and rings.

Continued

GRAPE CONSERVE

CONTINUED

8. Process the jars in a hot water bath (see page 31) for 5 minutes. Turn off the heat and let the jars rest in the water bath for 10 minutes.

9. Carefully remove the jars from the hot water canner. Set aside to cool for 12 hours.

10. Check the lids for proper seals (see page 32). Remove the rings, wipe the jars, label and date them, and transfer to a cupboard or pantry.

11. Refrigerate any jars that don't seal properly, and use within 3 weeks. Properly sealed jars will last in the cupboard for 12 months. Once opened, refrigerate and consume within 3 weeks.

PREPARATION TIP

If you've never skinned grapes before, don't worry. This is the easy way to learn. Concord grapes are a slip-skin grape. When squeezed, the grapes will just slip out of their skins.

PEAR BUTTER

MAKES 2 HALF-PINT JARS

WATER-BATH CANNING, LOW-SUGAR

There is something unforgettable about the glorious taste of pears gently cooked until their natural sugars thicken the fruit into a satisfying, deep brown, spreadable butter. Using a slow cooker is the easiest way to guarantee a great result. It is possible, though, to make this butter in a heavy-bottomed pot over very low heat. Choose the ripest pears you can find. A butter is the perfect way to use ripe fruit that isn't beautiful enough to poach or preserve whole; just cut away any bruised bits. You can substitute apples, peaches, plums, or apricots for some or all of the pears.

PREP TIME: 10 minutes
COOK TIME: 5 hours
PROCESSING TIME: 20 minutes
TOTAL TIME: 5 hours, 30 minutes

2 pounds pears, stemmed and cored
1/3 cup pear juice, or water
1/4 cup honey, or 3 tablespoons sugar (optional)
Juice of 1 lemon
Grated zest of 1 lemon

1. In a slow cooker or heavy-bottomed saucepot, combine the pears, pear juice, honey (if using), lemon juice, and lemon zest. Cook on the low setting, or over very low heat, for 5 hours, or until very thick.

2. Use a potato masher or a handheld blender to purée the pears until very smooth.

3. Prepare a hot water bath (see page 30). Place the jars in it to keep warm. Wash the lids and rings in hot, soapy water, and set aside.

4. Ladle the hot pear butter into the prepared jars, leaving 1/4 inch of headspace. Use a nonmetallic utensil to release any air bubbles. Wipe the rims clean and seal with the lids and rings.

5. Process the jars in a hot water bath (see page 31) for 20 minutes. Turn off the heat and let the jars rest in the water bath for 10 minutes.

Continued

PEAR BUTTER

CONTINUED

6. Carefully remove the jars from the hot water canner. Set aside to cool for 12 hours.

7. Check the lids for proper seals (see page 32). Remove the rings, wipe the jars, label and date them, and transfer to a cupboard or pantry.

8. Refrigerate any jars that don't seal properly, and use within 3 weeks. Properly sealed jars will last in the cupboard for 12 months. Once opened, refrigerate and consume within 3 weeks.

TRY INSTEAD

If you want a touch of spice in your pear butter, use whole spices tied in a cheesecloth sachet instead of ground spices, which might turn bitter during the long cooking time. For a batch this size, add a 1-inch slice of ginger, two or three whole cloves, or two small cinnamon sticks. It's usually best to add just one or two; more than that can overpower the pears. You can also boost the flavor by replacing the pear juice or water with a liqueur like Poire Williams brandy, or port.

SPICED APPLE BUTTER

MAKES 4 PINT JARS

WATER-BATH CANNING

Apple butter is a simple, firm spread that works as well on a piece of bread as it does served alongside pork or chicken. This is a basic recipe that can be adjusted to your liking for overall sweetness or the sweetness of different apples. For even more flavor, substitute pears for half of the apples to create pear-apple butter, or use a bumper crop of crabapples in this simple preparation.

PREP TIME: 20 minutes
COOK TIME: 2 hours
PROCESSING TIME: 10 minutes
TOTAL TIME: 2 hours, 30 minutes

4 pounds apples, roughly chopped (about 10 cups)
3 cups sugar
Juice of 1 lemon
2 tablespoons ground cinnamon
1 teaspoon ground nutmeg

1. Preheat the oven to 250°F.

2. In a Dutch oven set over a low heat, cook the apples for about 20 minutes, or until softened. For firm apples, you may need to add a bit of water to prevent scorching.

3. Using a food mill with a coarse screen, press the apples through to purée. Discard the cores and skins.

4. Prepare a hot water bath (see page 30). Place the jars in it to keep warm. Wash the lids and rings in hot, soapy water, and set aside.

5. Return the apples to the Dutch oven. Add the sugar, lemon juice, cinnamon, and nutmeg.

6. Uncovered, place the pot in the preheated oven until the apple mixture thickens. Cook for 1 to 2 hours, depending on the type of apples used. Stir every 20 minutes for the first hour, then every 10 minutes once the apple butter begins to thicken.

7. Ladle the apple butter into the prepared jars, leaving ¼ inch of headspace. Use a nonmetallic utensil to release any air bubbles. Wipe the rims clean and seal with the lids and rings.

8. Process the jars in a hot water bath (see page 31) for 10 minutes. Turn off the heat and let the jars rest in the water bath for 10 minutes.

Continued

SPICED APPLE BUTTER

CONTINUED

9. Carefully remove the jars from the hot water canner. Set aside to cool for 12 hours.

10. Check the lids for proper seals (see page 32). Remove the rings, wipe the jars, label and date them, and transfer to a cupboard or pantry.

11. Refrigerate any jars that don't seal properly, and use within 2 months. Properly sealed jars will last in the cupboard for 12 months. Once opened, refrigerate and consume within 2 months.

LOW-SUGAR PREPARATION TIP

To create a lower-sugar apple butter, simply decrease the amount of sugar by one cup or more, to taste. Additionally, other sweeteners such as honey or agave nectar can be used in the place of granulated sugar. Add the desired amount of sweeteners and adjust to taste. Keep in mind that the mixture will reduce considerably while cooking, concentrating the natural sugars present.

HEIRLOOM TOMATO BUTTER

MAKES 4 HALF-PINT JARS

WATER-BATH CANNING

Tomato butter may sound strange but, when canning, you can think outside the box to harvest the full bounty of summer's produce. This simple spread, made more easily with a slow cooker, is sweet and spiced, with the consistency of ketchup but a totally different flavor profile. Use it for dipping, as a glaze on meats, or on top of eggs for a summery taste.

PREP TIME: 15 minutes
COOK TIME: 12 hours, 30 minutes
PROCESSING TIME: 10 minutes
TOTAL TIME: 12 hours, 55 minutes

5 pounds heirloom tomatoes, cored and quartered
1 cinnamon stick
1 (1-inch) fresh ginger piece, peeled and sliced
1 tablespoon whole allspice berries
¼ teaspoon whole cloves
1½ cups honey
½ cup sugar
⅛ teaspoon cayenne pepper
2 tablespoons bottled lemon juice

1. In a large pot, mash the tomatoes with a potato masher to extract some of their juices. Bring to a boil over high heat. Cook for about 30 minutes, stirring occasionally, or until soft.

2. Using a food mill, pass the tomatoes through to remove the seeds and skins.

3. In a cheesecloth square, combine the cinnamon stick, ginger, allspice, and cloves. Tie securely with kitchen twine into a sachet.

4. In a slow cooker set to low, combine the tomato purée and the spice bag. Cover the slow cooker but slightly prop open the lid with a wooden spoon or other utensil so steam can escape as the purée reduces. Cook for about 12 hours, or until reduced by at least half.

5. Prepare a hot water bath (see page 30). Place the jars in it to keep warm. Wash the lids and rings in hot, soapy water, and set aside.

6. Add the honey, sugar, cayenne pepper, and lemon juice to the purée. Stir to combine.

7. Ladle the tomato butter into the prepared jars, leaving ¼ inch of headspace. Use a nonmetallic utensil to release any air bubbles. Wipe the rims clean and seal with the lids and rings.

8. Process the jars in a hot water bath (see page 31) for 10 minutes. Turn off the heat and let the jars rest in the water bath for 10 minutes.

Continued

HEIRLOOM TOMATO BUTTER

CONTINUED

9. Carefully remove the jars from the hot water canner. Set aside to cool for 12 hours.

10. Check the lids for proper seals (see page 32). Remove the rings, wipe the jars, label and date them, and transfer to a cupboard or pantry.

11. Refrigerate any jars that don't seal properly, and use within 2 months. Properly sealed jars will last in the cupboard for 12 months. Once opened, refrigerate and consume within 2 months.

LOW-SUGAR PREPARATION TIP

Depending on the sweetness of the tomatoes used, the amount of honey can be reduced to taste. Instead of adding the full amount, cut back to a ½ cup or 1 cup. If you prefer more sweetness, add a little more until you achieve the desired flavor.

DAMSON PLUM CHEESE

MAKES 8 HALF-PINT JARS, OR 4 PINT JARS

WATER-BATH CANNING

Damson plums are smaller than other plums, with a distinctive sour and bitter taste. They are loaded with pectin, so you don't need to add any additional. The extended cooking time turns this preparation from a soft spread into a sliceable cheese. It's the perfect accompaniment to cold roast meats, rich game birds like goose or duck, or a slice of perfectly aged farmhouse Cheddar.

PREP TIME: 10 minutes
COOK TIME: 2 hours
PROCESSING TIME: 20 minutes
TOTAL TIME: 2 hours, 30 minutes

2 pounds damson plums, stemmed
½ cup water
1¼ cups sugar
½ teaspoon freshly squeezed lemon juice

1. In a heavy-gauge saucepot or preserving pot set over medium heat, combine the plums and the water. Bring to a simmer. Cook for 1 to 1½ hours, or until the fruit is falling away from the stones.

2. Using a sieve or a food mill, push the plums through to purée.

3. In a preserving pot set over medium heat, combine the purée, sugar, and lemon juice. Bring to a simmer, stirring constantly. Reduce the heat to low. Simmer for about 30 minutes, or until the plums are very thick.

4. Prepare a hot water bath (see page 30). Place the jars in it to keep warm. Wash the lids and rings in hot, soapy water, and set aside.

5. Ladle the plum cheese into the prepared jars, leaving ¼ inch of headspace. Use a nonmetallic utensil to release any air bubbles. Wipe the rims clean and seal with the lids and rings.

6. Process the jars in a hot water bath (see page 31) for 20 minutes. Turn off the heat and let the jars rest in the water bath for 10 minutes.

7. Carefully remove the jars from the hot water canner. Set aside to cool for 12 hours.

8. Check the lids for proper seals (see page 32). Remove the rings, wipe the jars, label and date them, and transfer to a cupboard or pantry.

9. Refrigerate any jars that don't seal properly, and use within 6 weeks. Properly sealed jars will last in the cupboard for 12 months. Once opened, refrigerate and consume within 6 weeks.

PLUM AND QUINCE MEMBRILLO

MAKES 4 HALF-PINT JARS

WATER-BATH CANNING, SEASONAL

Membrillo is a specialty preserve made in Spain and Portugal. Traditionally, the recipe uses only quince, but the addition of plum gives it a delicious fruitiness. The quince provides enough pectin to set this preserve into a paste that is firm enough to slice. The classic way to serve *membrillo* is as an accompaniment to the salty sheep's milk manchego cheese. Try it in sandwiches or with sliced cold meats, especially pork.

PREP TIME: 30 minutes
COOK TIME: 1 hour, 15 minutes
PROCESSING TIME: 10 minutes
TOTAL TIME: 1 hour, 55 minutes

4½ pounds quince, peeled, cored, and thinly sliced; peels, cores, and seeds reserved
2¼ pounds black plums, pitted and quartered
4½ cups granulated sugar, plus additional as needed
3 tablespoons freshly squeezed lemon juice
3 strips (½-inch wide and 1-inch long) lemon peel, pith removed
1 cinnamon stick

1. Prepare a hot water bath (see page 30). Place the jars in it to keep warm. Wash the lids and rings in hot, soapy water, and set aside.

2. In a cheesecloth square, combine the reserved quince peels, cores, and seeds. Tie securely with kitchen twine into a sachet.

3. In a preserving pot or a deep pot set over medium heat, combine the quince, plums, and sachet. Add enough water to cover the fruit and the sachet. Simmer for about 45 minutes, stirring frequently and adding water as needed to keep the quince from drying out, until the quince is very tender and red.

4. Remove from the heat. Remove and discard the sachet.

5. Use a potato masher to purée the quince and plums into a smooth paste.

6. Add the sugar, lemon juice, lemon peel, and cinnamon stick. Return to a simmer over low heat. Cook for about 30 minutes, stirring frequently, or until the mixture is thick enough to leave a track when a spoon is dragged through it. Remove and discard the cinnamon stick.

7. Ladle the *membrillo* into the prepared jars, leaving ¼ inch of headspace. Use a nonmetallic utensil to release any air bubbles. Wipe the rims clean and seal with the lids and rings.

8. Process the jars in a hot water bath (see page 31) for 10 minutes. Turn off the heat and let the jars rest in the water bath for 10 minutes.

9. Carefully remove the jars from the hot water canner. Set aside to cool for 12 hours.

10. Check the lids for proper seals (see page 32). Remove the rings, wipe the jars, label and date them, and transfer to a cupboard or pantry.

11. Refrigerate any jars that don't seal properly, and use within 2 months. Properly sealed jars will last in the cupboard for 12 months. Once opened, refrigerate and consume within 2 months.

PAIR IT

For a party presentation, slice the *membrillo* into squares and roll in granulated sugar. Serve alongside a variety of salty or blue cheeses, or pair with Spanish cheeses such as manchego, Roncal, or Mahón.

LEMON CURD

MAKES 2 HALF-PINT JARS

WATER-BATH CANNING

Lemon curd is a bright, tangy custard that pairs delightfully with cakes, tarts, breads, and scones. If you don't have a double boiler, improvise with a heat-proof mixing bowl set over a saucepan filled with water to produce identical, uniformly creamy results. If you have access to fresh, pastured eggs, by all means use them here as their brighter yolks will create a supremely yellow result.

PREP TIME: 10 minutes
COOK TIME: 20 minutes
PROCESSING TIME: 25 minutes
TOTAL TIME: 55 minutes

3 large egg yolks
2 large eggs
⅔ cup freshly squeezed lemon juice, strained
6 tablespoons unsalted butter, at room temperature
1 cup sugar
2 tablespoons grated lemon zest

1. Prepare a hot water bath (see page 30). Place the jars in it to keep warm. Wash the lids and rings in hot, soapy water, and set aside.

2. Fill a double boiler with about 2 inches of water and simmer over medium heat.

3. In a medium bowl, beat the egg yolks and eggs together. Add the lemon juice and mix well.

4. To the top of the double boiler, add the butter and stir until melted. Add the sugar and mix to combine. Add the eggs and continue stirring.

5. Continue to cook, stirring constantly. The lemon curd will begin to thicken after about 5 minutes. Once it reaches about 190°F, measured with a candy thermometer, or rounds up on a spoon, the thickening should be noticeable. *It should not boil.*

6. Continue stirring, maintaining the temperature for 6 to 8 minutes more, or until it is the consistency of yogurt. Turn off the heat.

7. Stir in the lemon zest.

8. Ladle the lemon curd into the prepared jars, leaving ½ inch of headspace. Use a nonmetallic utensil to release any air bubbles. Wipe the rims clean and seal with the lids and rings.

9. Process the jars in a hot water bath (see page 31) for 25 minutes. Turn off the heat and let the jars rest in the water bath for 10 minutes.

10. Carefully remove the jars from the hot water canner. Set aside to cool for 12 hours.

11. Check the lids for proper seals (see page 32). Remove the rings, wipe the jars, label and date them, and transfer to a cupboard or pantry.

12. Refrigerate any jars that don't seal properly, and use within 2 months. Properly sealed jars will last in the cupboard for 12 months. Once opened, refrigerate and consume within 2 months.

PREPARATION TIP

Use a Microplane grater to create finely grated lemon zest for this recipe. Otherwise, the end product will have an undesirable consistency. If you don't have a Microplane grater, add the lemon zest to the sugar and cook the lemon curd with the zest. When it is finished, press the lemon curd through a wire mesh strainer with the back of a spoon to remove the zest and produce a creamy lemon curd.

LIME CURD

MAKES 2 HALF-PINT JARS

WATER-BATH CANNING

While lemon curd is a well-known English treat, lime curd evokes a feel of the Caribbean simply with its delightful aroma. Great on yogurt, a biscuit, or a tart, this simple treat is a great way to break up the monotony of a long winter.

PREP TIME: 20 minutes
COOK TIME: 20 minutes
PROCESSING TIME: 25 minutes
TOTAL TIME: 1 hour, 5 minutes

3 large egg yolks
2 large eggs
⅔ cup freshly squeezed lime juice, strained
6 tablespoons unsalted butter, at room temperature
1 cup sugar
2 tablespoons grated lime zest

1. Prepare a hot water bath (see page 30). Place the jars in it to keep warm. Wash the lids and rings in hot, soapy water, and set aside.

2. Fill a double boiler with about 2 inches of water and simmer over medium heat.

3. In a separate bowl, beat the egg yolks and eggs together. Add the lime juice and mix well.

4. To the top of the double boiler, add the butter and stir until melted. Add the sugar and mix to combine. Add the eggs and continue stirring.

5. Continue to cook, stirring constantly. The lime curd will begin to thicken after about 5 minutes. Once it reaches about 190°F, measured with a candy thermometer, and rounds up on a spoon, the thickening should be noticeable. Continue stirring for about 10 minutes more, or until the consistency of yogurt.

6. Stir in the lime zest.

7. Ladle the lime curd into the prepared jars, leaving ½ inch of headspace. Use a nonmetallic utensil to release any air bubbles. Wipe the rims clean and seal with the lids and rings.

8. Process the jars in a hot water bath (see page 31) for 25 minutes. Turn off the heat and let the jars rest in the water bath for 10 minutes.

9. Carefully remove the jars from the hot water canner. Set aside to cool for 12 hours.

10. Check the lids for proper seals (see page 32). Remove the rings, wipe the jars, label and date them, and transfer to a cupboard or pantry.

11. Refrigerate any jars that don't seal properly, and use within 2 months. Properly sealed jars will last in the cupboard for 12 months. Once opened, refrigerate and consume within 2 months.

CUPS

5

FILLINGS, SYRUPS, SAUCES & CONDIMENTS

There is nothing like opening a jar of homemade pie filling in the dead of winter and having a pie in the oven in minutes. The same convenience comes when making tomato sauce, ketchup, and the myriad of fruit and vegetable sauces, syrups, and condiments in this chapter. Stock your shelves with these necessities now, and skip the trips to the store later.

APPLE PIE FILLING

MAKES 2 QUART JARS

WATER-BATH CANNING

This combination of apples and spices will tempt you to bake the perfect apple pie, no matter what the season. A single quart container fills a 9-inch pie perfectly.

PREP TIME: 20 minutes
COOK TIME: 10 minutes
PROCESSING TIME: 30 minutes
TOTAL TIME: 1 hour

4 pounds fresh apples, cored, peeled, and cut into ¼-inch-thick wedges (about 10 cups)
1 ¾ cups sugar
½ cup ClearJel (See Glossary, page 240)
1 ½ cups apple juice
1 cup cold water
¼ cup bottled lemon juice
1 teaspoon ground cinnamon
¼ teaspoon ground nutmeg (optional)

1. Bring a large pot of water to a rolling boil over high heat.

2. Add the apples. Cook for about 4 minutes, or until they just start to turn translucent. Drain in a colander. Set aside.

3. In a preserving pot or deep pot set over medium-high heat, stir together the sugar and ClearJel. Add the apple juice, water, lemon juice, cinnamon, and nutmeg (if using). Bring to a simmer, stirring to dissolve the sugar completely.

4. Add the apples. Continue simmering for about 5 minutes, or until the apples are very hot. Remove from the heat and cool to room temperature.

5. Prepare a hot water bath (see page 30). Place the jars in it to keep warm. Wash the lids and rings in hot, soapy water, and set aside.

6. Ladle the hot filling into the prepared jars, leaving 1 inch of headspace. Use a nonmetallic utensil to remove any air bubbles. Wipe the rims clean and seal with the lids and rings.

7. Process the jars in a hot water bath (see page 31) for 30 minutes. Turn off the heat and let the jars rest in the water bath for 10 minutes.

8. Carefully remove the jars from the hot water canner. Set aside to cool for 12 hours. Check the lids for proper seals (see page 32). Remove the rings, wipe the jars clean, label and date them, and transfer to a cupboard or pantry for up to 12 months.

9. Refrigerate any jars that don't seal properly, and use within 3 weeks. Properly sealed jars will last in the cupboard for 12 months. Once opened, refrigerate and consume within 3 weeks.

SOUR CHERRY PIE FILLING

MAKES 2 QUART JARS

WATER-BATH CANNING, SEASONAL

Sour cherries have a very short season and are difficult to find frozen. Tart or sour cherry juice was previously found only in health food stores, but is more widely available now. Use only real juice, not one made from concentrate. If you can't find the real thing, using water is fine but the juice will add a bold flavor to your finished filling.

PREP TIME: 25 minutes
COOK TIME: 10 minutes
PROCESSING TIME: 30 minutes
TOTAL TIME: 1 hour, 5 minutes

2 1/4 cups sugar
2/3 cup ClearJel (See Glossary, page 240)
1 1/2 cups sour cherry juice, or water
1/4 cup bottled lemon juice
1/2 teaspoon almond extract (optional)
4 1/2 pounds sour cherries, peeled and pitted (about 12 cups)

1. In a preserving pot or deep pot set over medium-high heat, stir together the sugar and ClearJel. Add the cherry juice, lemon juice, and almond extract (if using). Bring to a simmer, cook for 4 minutes, stirring to dissolve the sugar completely, and until very thick.

2. Add the cherries. Continue simmering for about 2 minutes, or until the cherries are very hot. Remove the pot from the heat and cool to room temperature.

3. Prepare a hot water bath (see page 30). Place the jars in it to keep warm. Wash the lids and rings in hot, soapy water, and set aside.

4. Ladle the hot filling into the prepared jars, leaving 1 inch of headspace. Use a nonmetallic utensil to remove any air bubbles. Wipe the rims clean and seal with the lids and rings.

5. Process the jars in a hot water bath (see page 31) for 30 minutes. Turn off the heat and let the jars rest in the water bath for 10 minutes.

6. Carefully remove the jars from the hot water canner. Set aside to cool for 12 hours.

7. Check the lids for proper seals (see page 32). Remove the rings, wipe the jars clean, label and date them, and store in a dark cupboard or pantry for up to 12 months.

8. Refrigerate any jars that don't seal properly, and use within 3 weeks. Properly sealed jars will last in the cupboard for 12 months. Once opened, refrigerate and consume within 3 weeks.

PEACH PIE FILLING

MAKES 2 QUART JARS

WATER-BATH CANNING

There is nothing like baking—and eating—a fresh peach pie in the dead of winter. All you need is a jar of this delicious filling. Simply make a double crust (or pick one up from the grocery store), pour the filling in the bottom, top and seal with the second crust, and toss the pie in the oven for a quick, summer-filled dessert.

PREP TIME: 30 minutes
COOK TIME: 5 minutes
PROCESSING TIME: 30 minutes
TOTAL TIME: 1 hour, 5 minutes

7 cups peeled, sliced peaches
2 cups sugar
1½ cups water
½ cup plus 2 tablespoons ClearJel (See Glossary, page 240)
1 teaspoon pure vanilla extract
½ teaspoon ground cinnamon
½ cup bottled lemon juice

1. Prepare a hot water bath (see page 30). Place the jars in it to keep warm. Wash the lids and rings in hot, soapy water, and set aside.

2. Bring a large pot of water to a boil. Submerge the peaches in the water. When the water returns to a boil, set a timer for 1 minute. Drain the peaches in a colander. Set aside.

3. In a large pot over high heat, combine the sugar, water, ClearJel, vanilla, and cinnamon. Bring to a boil. Add the lemon juice. Continue to cook for 1 minute more.

4. Fold in the peach slices. Cook, for 3 minutes, stirring constantly. Turn off the heat.

5. Ladle the hot filling into the prepared jars, leaving 1 inch of headspace. Use a nonmetallic utensil to release any air bubbles. Wipe the rims clean and seal with the lids and rings.

6. Process the jars in a hot water bath (see page 31) for 30 minutes. Turn off the heat and let the jars rest in the water bath for 10 minutes.

7. Carefully remove the jars from the hot water canner. Set aside to cool for 12 hours.

8. Check the lids for proper seals (see page 32). Remove the rings, wipe the jars, label and date them, and transfer to a cupboard or pantry.

9. Refrigerate any jars that don't seal properly, and use within 3 weeks. Properly sealed jars will last in the cupboard for 12 months. Once opened, refrigerate and consume within 3 weeks.

CLOSER LOOK

To peel peaches, bring a large pot of water to a boil and prepare an ice bath. Cut an "X" into the skin of each peach. Add them to the boiling water in batches. Blanch for 1 to 2 minutes, or until the skins begin to curl. With a slotted spoon, remove the peaches from the pot and transfer to the ice bath to cool. After 1 to 2 minutes of cooling, slip the skins off, cut the peaches in half, remove the pit, and they're ready to use.

PEAR HONEY

MAKES 6 HALF-PINT JARS

WATER-BATH CANNING

There is no mistake in the ingredients—there is no honey in this recipe. The recipe's name refers to the fact that the pears are cooked down to a rich, honey-like syrup. The lengthy cooking time turns this into a thick, gooey preserve. Old-time recipes call for slightly under-ripe, firm green pears. The most likely source for these is your own tree or a generous neighbor with a tree. Failing that, locate a pick-your-own orchard. Don't fret, though, if you aren't sure exactly how ripe your pears are.

PREP TIME: 20 minutes
COOK TIME: 5 hours
PROCESSING TIME: 10 minutes
TOTAL TIME: 5 hours, 30 minutes

4½ pounds pears, cored and finely chopped
5 cups sugar
4 cups canned crushed pineapple

1. In a slow cooker or heavy-gauge saucepot, combine the pears, sugar, and pineapple. Cook for 5 hours on the low setting, or over very low heat, until very thick. Stir occasionally.

2. Prepare a hot water bath (see page 30). Place the jars in it to keep warm. Wash the lids and rings in hot, soapy water, and set aside.

3. Ladle the hot pear honey into the prepared jars, leaving ¼ inch of headspace. Use a nonmetallic utensil to release any air bubbles. Wipe the rims clean and seal with the lids and rings.

4. Process the jars in a hot water bath (see page 31) for 10 minutes. Turn off the heat and let the jars rest in the water bath for 10 minutes.

5. Carefully remove the jars from the hot water canner. Set aside to cool for 12 hours.

6. Check the lids for proper seals (see page 32). Remove the rings, wipe the jars, label and date them, and transfer to a cupboard or pantry.

7. Refrigerate any jars that don't seal properly, and use within 3 weeks. Properly sealed jars will last in the cupboard for 12 months. Once opened, refrigerate and consume within 3 weeks.

PREPARATION TIP

Chopping all those pears by hand can be a chore. You can use a meat grinder or food processor to get the job done more quickly.

PEACH NECTAR

MAKES 5 PINT JARS

WATER-BATH CANNING

Fresh peaches, simmered in sweet syrup and puréed into a pourable drink, are transformed into nectar here. Use either yellow or white peaches, then mix with a sparkling wine like prosecco or cava for a change from mimosas at brunch. It also makes a great summertime drink, chilled until icy cold. Add to a pitcher of lemonade or iced tea and garnish with lime wedges and mint for a new take on summer's soft drinks.

PREP TIME: 15 minutes
COOK TIME: 15 minutes, plus 15 minutes cooling time
PROCESSING TIME: 15 minutes
TOTAL TIME: 1 hour

2 pounds peaches, peeled, pitted, and chopped (about 4 cups)
1 cup water
½ cup sugar, plus additional as needed
1 tablespoon freshly squeezed lemon juice, plus additional as needed

1. Prepare a hot water bath (see page 30). Place the jars in it to keep warm. Wash the lids and rings in hot, soapy water, and set aside.

2. In a preserving pot or a deep pot set over medium heat, combine the peaches and water. Bring to a simmer. Cook for about 10 minutes, or until the peaches are soft enough to mash easily. Remove from the heat and let cool for 15 minutes.

3. Using a blender or food processor, purée the peaches in batches. Return them to the pot and bring to a simmer over medium heat.

4. Add the sugar and lemon juice to taste. Bring to a full rolling boil. Cook for about 5 minutes, or until the sugar dissolves.

5. Ladle the hot peach nectar into the prepared jars, leaving ¼ inch of headspace. Use a nonmetallic utensil to release any air bubbles. Wipe the rims clean and seal with the lids and rings.

6. Process the jars in a hot water bath (see page 31) for 15 minutes. Turn off the heat and let the jars rest in the water bath for 10 minutes.

7. Carefully remove the jars from the hot water canner. Set aside to cool for 12 hours.

8. Check the lids for proper seals (see page 32). Remove the rings, wipe the jars, label and date them, and transfer to a cupboard or pantry.

9. Refrigerate any jars that don't seal properly, and use within 3 weeks. Properly sealed jars will last in the cupboard for 12 months. Once opened, refrigerate and consume within 3 weeks.

RHUBARB SYRUP WITH VANILLA AND CARDAMOM

MAKES 4 HALF-PINT JARS

WATER-BATH CANNING

This refreshing syrup is perfect for sweetening iced tea or other cold drinks, or as the base for a cocktail. You can skip the canning process and simply refrigerate the syrup in a clean jar or bottle where it will last about three weeks. If you are lucky enough to have frozen rhubarb from your garden, pull some out in the dead of winter, make this syrup, and enjoy the freshness of spring.

PREP TIME: 15 minutes
COOK TIME: 15 minutes, plus 1 hour straining time
PROCESSING TIME: 15 minutes
TOTAL TIME: 1 hour, 45 minutes

2 pounds fresh or frozen rhubarb, ends trimmed and cut into 1-inch chunks (about 6 cups)
1½ cups water, plus additional as needed
3 cups sugar
⅓ cup freshly squeezed lemon juice
3 cardamom pods
½ vanilla bean, split lengthwise, seeds scraped out, bean and seeds reserved

1. In a large saucepot set over medium heat, combine the rhubarb and 1½ cups of water. Bring to a boil. Cook for about 10 minutes, or until the rhubarb breaks down into shreds.

2. Suspend a jelly bag over a bowl, or line a colander with a triple layer of rinsed cheesecloth. Add the rhubarb and strain for about 1 hour, without pressing or squeezing, for the clearest syrup. Measure 3 cups of juice, adding water to make up the difference, if needed. If you have more than 3 cups of juice, make a second batch or save for another use.

3. Prepare a hot water bath (see page 30). Place the jars in it to keep warm. Wash the lids and rings in hot, soapy water, and set aside.

4. In a preserving pot or saucepot, combine the rhubarb juice, sugar, lemon juice, cardamom pods, vanilla bean, and vanilla seeds.

5. Bring to a simmer over medium-high heat, stirring until the sugar dissolves, about 1 minute. Continue to simmer for another 5 minutes, or until the syrup is slightly thickened. Remove and discard the cardamom pods. Remove the vanilla bean, which can be reserved, gently rinsed and dried, and used to scent sugar or for another recipe.

6. Ladle the hot rhubarb syrup into the prepared jars, leaving ¼ inch of headspace. Use a nonmetallic utensil to release any air bubbles. Wipe the rims clean and seal with the lids and rings.

7. Process the jars in a hot water bath (see page 31) for 15 minutes. Turn off the heat and let the jars rest in the water bath for 10 minutes.

8. Carefully remove the jars from the hot water canner. Set aside to cool for 12 hours.

9. Check the lids for proper seals (see page 32). Remove the rings, wipe the jars, label and date them, and transfer to a cupboard or pantry.

10. Refrigerate any jars that don't seal properly, and use within 3 weeks. Properly sealed jars will last in the cupboard for 12 months. Once opened, refrigerate and consume within 3 weeks.

RASPBERRY-LEMON SYRUP

MAKES 4 HALF-PINT JARS

WATER-BATH CANNING

Use this syrup as a topping on pancakes, or mix it with spirits or sparkling water to create cocktails and "mocktails." Simple to make, fruit syrups are an economical alternative to real maple syrup and don't disappoint in flavor. As a bonus, these easy syrups can be made from frozen fruits, so hide away a few extra pints in your freezer to brighten those dark winter days.

PREP TIME: 5 minutes
COOK TIME: 15 minutes, plus 2 to 3 hours draining time
PROCESSING TIME: 10 minutes
TOTAL TIME: 3 hours, 30 minutes

3 pints fresh raspberries
3 cups water
Zest of 1 lemon
2 cups sugar
Juice of 1 lemon

1. Prepare a hot water bath (see page 30). Place the jars in it to keep warm. Wash the lids and rings in hot, soapy water, and set aside.

2. In a small pot set over medium heat, combine the raspberries, water, and lemon zest. Bring to a boil. Reduce the heat to low. Simmer for 10 minutes.

3. Place a wire mesh strainer over a bowl. Pour in the raspberry mixture to drain. Do not press the raspberries, as this results in a cloudy syrup. Once the dripping ceases, after 2 to 3 hours, discard the solids.

4. Rinse the pot, return it to the stove, and pour in the raspberry juice. Add the sugar and lemon juice. Bring to a boil over high heat. Turn off the heat and skim off any foam.

5. Ladle the hot syrup into the prepared jars, leaving ½ inch of headspace. Use a nonmetallic utensil to release any air bubbles. Wipe the rims clean and seal with the lids and rings.

6. Process the jars in a hot water bath (see page 31) for 10 minutes. Turn off the heat and let the jars rest in the water bath for 10 minutes.

7. Carefully remove the jars from the hot water canner. Set aside to cool for 12 hours.

8. Check the lids for proper seals (see page 32). Remove the rings, wipe the jars, label and date them, and transfer to a cupboard or pantry.

9. Refrigerate any jars that don't seal properly, and use within 3 weeks. Properly sealed jars will last in the cupboard for 12 months. Once opened, refrigerate and consume within 3 weeks.

CLOSER LOOK

Raspberries are a delicate fruit best handled with care. They are especially prone to mold and rot. When picking, keep them clean so you don't have to rinse them. If not using right away, refrigerate them in a single layer for a day or two, or freeze them in a single layer and transfer to a storage container once solid.

BLACKBERRY-SAGE SYRUP

MAKES 4 HALF-PINT JARS

WATER-BATH CANNING

Blackberry and sage is a combination that works spectacularly in cocktails, as the savory sage plays well off the sweet blackberry. Use this dark, rich syrup to top yogurt or waffles for an imaginative twist on the ordinary. Blackberries are a late-summer seasonal delight that can be found both at markets and in the wild throughout much of the country.

PREP TIME: 10 minutes
COOK TIME: 15 minutes
PROCESSING TIME: 10 minutes
TOTAL TIME: 35 minutes

3 pints fresh blackberries
3 cups water
20 to 30 sage leaves, torn in half
2 cups sugar

1. Prepare a hot water bath (see page 30). Place the jars in it to keep warm. Wash the lids and rings in hot, soapy water, and set aside.

2. In a small pot set over high heat, combine the blackberries, water, and sage leaves. Bring to a boil. Reduce the heat to medium. Simmer the mixture for 10 minutes.

3. Place a wire mesh strainer over a bowl. Pour in the blackberry mixture to drain. Do not press the blackberries, as this results in a cloudy syrup. Once the dripping ceases, discard the solids.

4. Rinse the pot, return it to the stove over medium-high heat, and pour in the blackberry juice.

5. Add the sugar. Bring to a boil. Turn off the heat and skim off any foam.

6. Ladle the hot syrup into the prepared jars, leaving ½ inch of headspace. Use a nonmetallic utensil to release any air bubbles. Wipe the rims clean and seal with the lids and rings.

7. Process the jars in a hot water bath (see page 31) for 10 minutes. Turn off the heat and let the jars rest in the water bath for 10 minutes.

8. Carefully remove the jars from the hot water canner. Set aside to cool for 12 hours.

9. Check the lids for proper seals (see page 32). Remove the rings, wipe the jars, label and date them, and transfer to a cupboard or pantry.

10. Refrigerate any jars that don't seal properly, and use within 3 weeks. Properly sealed jars will last in the cupboard for 12 months. Once opened, refrigerate and consume within 3 weeks.

DID YOU KNOW?

Sage is a culinary herb also known for its medicinal properties. It has long been used to treat sore throats, coughs, and fevers. Sage is also a well-known therapy to treat digestive upset and is thought to help increase brain function and memory. While sage leaves should not be canned because they tend to turn bitter, this infusion works well as a canned syrup.

APPLESAUCE

MAKES 4 PINT JARS

WATER-BATH CANNING, LOW-SUGAR

Different apple varieties have different characteristics. The varieties most often suggested for cooking and making sauce are Golden Delicious, McIntosh, Grimes Golden, Cortland, and Jonathan, but you can use whatever variety you have or prefer. Keep your apples in a large bowl of water and lemon juice to prevent them from turning brown after they've been cut. If you'd like to give your applesauce a lovely pink hue, leave the red skins on your apples as they cook.

PREP TIME: 25 minutes
COOK TIME: 10 minutes
PROCESSING TIME: 15 minutes
TOTAL TIME: 50 minutes

¼ cup freshly squeezed lemon juice (see above)
6 pounds apples, cored and quartered, peeling optional
1½ cups water, plus additional as needed
1½ cups granulated sugar (optional)

1. Prepare a hot water bath (see page 30). Place the jars in it to keep warm. Wash the lids and rings in hot, soapy water, and set aside.

2. Drain the apples from the lemon water.

3. In a preserving pot or deep pot set over medium heat, combine the apples and 1½ cups of water. Simmer for about 10 minutes, stirring frequently, or until the fruit is very tender and starting to fall apart.

4. Add the sugar to taste (if using). Remove the pot from the heat.

5. Using a sieve, push the apples through to purée.

6. Ladle the applesauce into the prepared jars, leaving ½ inch of headspace. Use a nonmetallic utensil to release any air bubbles. Wipe the rims clean and seal with the lids and rings.

7. Process the jars in a hot water bath (see page 31) for 15 minutes. Turn off the heat and let the jars rest in the water bath for 10 minutes.

8. Carefully remove the jars from the hot water canner. Set aside to cool for 12 hours.

9. Check the lids for proper seals (see page 32). Remove the rings, wipe the jars, label and date them, and transfer to a cupboard or pantry.

10. Refrigerate any jars that don't seal properly, and use within 3 weeks. Properly sealed jars will last in the cupboard for 12 months. Once opened, refrigerate and consume within 3 weeks.

TRY INSTEAD

Cinnamon is always a nice addition to applesauce. If you want a touch of spice, add a cinnamon stick to the apples as they simmer, then remove it before you purée the sauce. Ginger, lemon and orange zest, and cloves can also be used to season the applesauce.

SPICED APPLE-PEAR SAUCE

MAKES 5 PINT JARS

WATER-BATH CANNING, LOW-SUGAR

Apples alone make a versatile sauce. Apple-pear sauce provides a grown-up taste all its own. Using no sugar, this recipe relies on the sweetness of the fruits only and a few spices to liven the palate. This sauce just begs to be eaten on almost anything.

PREP TIME: 25 minutes
COOK TIME: 35 minutes
PROCESSING TIME: 15 minutes
TOTAL TIME: 1 hour, 15 minutes

3 pounds apples, roughly chopped
3 pounds pears, roughly chopped
1 ½ cups water
2 teaspoons ground cinnamon
½ teaspoon ground cloves
½ teaspoon ground allspice

1. Prepare a hot water bath (see page 30). Place the jars in it to keep warm. Wash the lids and rings in hot, soapy water, and set aside.

2. In a large pot set over medium-high heat, combine the apples, pears, and water. Bring to a boil. Reduce the heat to medium. Simmer for about 30 minutes, or until the apples and pears are very soft.

3. Using a food mill, pass the apples and pears through to purée. Discard the cores and skins.

4. Rinse the pot, return it to the stove, and pour in the puréed sauce. Return the sauce to a boil over medium-high heat. Cook for 5 minutes.

5. Stir in the cinnamon, cloves, and allspice.

6. Ladle the hot apple-pear sauce into the prepared jars, leaving ½ inch of headspace. Use a nonmetallic utensil to release any air bubbles. Wipe the rims clean and seal with the lids and rings.

7. Process the jars in a hot water bath (see page 31) for 15 minutes. Turn off the heat and let the jars rest in the water bath for 10 minutes.

8. Carefully remove the jars from the hot water canner. Set aside to cool for 12 hours.

9. Check the lids for proper seals (see page 32). Remove the rings, wipe the jars, label and date them, and transfer to a cupboard or pantry.

10. Refrigerate any jars that don't seal properly, and use within 3 weeks. Properly sealed jars will last in the cupboard for 12 months. Once opened, refrigerate and consume within 3 weeks.

TRY INSTEAD

If you don't have a food mill, you can still make this, and other sauces, but it will take more time. Peel and core the apples. After cooking, simply purée the fruit in a blender or food processor. For a chunkier sauce, mash the cooked apples and pears with a potato masher.

CRANBERRY SAUCE

MAKES 4 HALF-PINT JARS, OR 2 PINT JARS

WATER-BATH CANNING

This sauce is made with whole cranberries and is meant to be a little looser than the cranberry sauce you plop from a can and slice. It should have some gel, though, thanks to all the pectin and acid found naturally in cranberries. Serve this sauce as a spread on cold meat sandwiches, on its own, stirred into mayonnaise, or added to a chicken salad for a "berry" good treat.

PREP TIME: 5 minutes
COOK TIME: 20 minutes
PROCESSING TIME: 15 minutes
TOTAL TIME: 40 minutes

2 cups granulated sugar
2 cups water
1 pound fresh cranberries (about 4 cups)
2 teaspoons grated orange zest (optional)

1. Prepare a hot water bath (see page 30). Place the jars in it to keep warm. Wash the lids and rings in hot, soapy water, and set aside.

2. In a small saucepan set over high heat, combine the sugar and water. Stir until the mixture comes to a boil. Continue boiling for 5 minutes.

3. Add the cranberries and return to a boil. Reduce the heat to medium. Simmer for 10 to 15 minutes, stirring frequently, until the berries burst and the mixture reaches 220°F, measured with a candy thermometer. Test for gel after 10 minutes (see page 32).

4. Stir in the orange zest (if using).

5. Ladle the hot cranberry sauce into the prepared jars, leaving ¼ inch of headspace. Use a nonmetallic utensil to release any air bubbles. Wipe the rims clean and seal with the lids and rings.

6. Process the jars in a hot water bath (see page 31) for 15 minutes. Turn off the heat and let the jars rest in the water bath for 10 minutes.

7. Carefully remove the jars from the hot water canner. Set aside to cool for 12 hours.

8. Check the lids for proper seals (see page 32). Remove the rings, wipe the jars, label and date them, and transfer to a cupboard or pantry.

9. Refrigerate any jars that don't seal properly, and use within 3 weeks. Properly sealed jars will last in the cupboard for 12 months. Once opened, refrigerate and consume within 3 weeks.

GREEN MANGO SAUCE

MAKES 6 HALF-PINT JARS

WATER-BATH CANNING

Green mangos are simply underripe mangos, which are usually easy to find at the market. They can irritate your skin the same way poison ivy can, as they are part of the same family. Protect yourself by wearing kitchen gloves while working with this fruit. Don't touch your face, lips, or eyes after touching or cutting raw green mangos, and wash your hands and utensils thoroughly afterward to remove all traces. Once cooked, the mangos lose their ability to make you itch. If this sauce is exposed to direct sunlight it can lose its beautiful color, so keep it in a dark cupboard.

PREP TIME: 25 minutes
COOK TIME: 25 minutes
PROCESSING TIME: 10 minutes
TOTAL TIME: 1 hour

5 pounds green mangos, peeled and cubed
¾ cup sugar
6 tablespoons honey
¼ cup bottled lemon juice
⅛ teaspoon ground cinnamon
⅛ teaspoon ground nutmeg
3 teaspoons citric acid, divided

1. Prepare a hot water bath (see page 30). Place the jars in it to keep warm. Wash the lids and rings in hot, soapy water, and set aside.

2. In a preserving pot or a saucepot set over medium heat, combine the mangos, sugar, honey, lemon juice, cinnamon, and nutmeg. Bring to a simmer. Cook for 20 to 25 minutes, stirring frequently, until the sugar dissolves and the mangos are tender enough to mash easily. Remove from the heat and cool for a few minutes.

3. Using a sieve, a food processor, or blender, pass the mangos through to purée. Return the sauce to the saucepot and return to a simmer.

4. Add ½ teaspoon of citric acid to each jar.

5. Ladle the hot mango sauce into the prepared jars, leaving ¼ inch of headspace. Use a nonmetallic utensil to release any air bubbles. Wipe the rims clean and seal with the lids and rings.

6. Process the jars in a hot water bath (see page 31) for 10 minutes. Turn off the heat and let the jars rest in the water bath for 10 minutes.

7. Carefully remove the jars from the hot water canner. Set aside to cool for 12 hours.

8. Check the lids for proper seals (see page 32). Remove the rings, wipe the jars, label and date them, and transfer to a cupboard or pantry.

9. Refrigerate any jars that don't seal properly, and use within 3 weeks. Properly sealed jars will last in the cupboard for 12 months. Once opened, refrigerate and consume within 3 weeks.

CLASSIC TOMATO SAUCE WITH VARIATIONS

MAKES 8 PINT JARS, OR 4 QUART JARS

WATER-BATH CANNING, LOW-SUGAR, LOW-SODIUM

This recipe is essentially a concentrated essence of tomatoes with nothing else added, allowing you the most flexibility to adjust seasonings later on. Taste the sauce when it has the texture you prefer and make adjustments to the flavor, if needed. Very ripe tomatoes won't need any sweetening. If your sauce tastes bitter, add a pinch of salt to balance it; if it tastes too sour, add a pinch of sugar; and, if it is too sweet, add a few drops of red wine vinegar.

PREP TIME: 35 minutes
COOK TIME: 1 hour, 5 minutes
PROCESSING TIME: 35 minutes for pint jars; 40 minutes for quart jars
TOTAL TIME: 2 hours, 20 minutes

18 pounds tomatoes, stemmed and chopped
Salt, for seasoning (optional)
Sugar, for seasoning (optional)
Red wine vinegar, for seasoning (optional)
2 teaspoons citric acid, divided

1. To a large saucepot (you may need two pots) set over medium heat, add the tomatoes in batches, crushing them with a potato masher or a wooden spoon until all are incorporated. Bring to a simmer. Cook for about 5 minutes, stirring frequently, or until very tender.

2. Using a food mill or mesh sieve, strain the tomatoes into a clean saucepot. Use a spatula to press out as much sauce as possible. Discard the skin and seeds.

3. Bring the pot to a simmer over medium heat. Continue to simmer for 45 minutes to 1 hour or longer, stirring frequently, until the sauce is reduced by one-third for a thin sauce, or one-half for a thick sauce. Taste the sauce and season with salt (if using), sugar (if using), and/or red wine vinegar (if using).

4. Prepare a hot water bath (see page 30). Place the jars in it to keep warm. Wash the lids and rings in hot, soapy water, and set aside.

5. Spoon citric acid into each prepared jar: ¼ teaspoon into each pint jar, or ½ teaspoon into each quart jar. Ladle the hot sauce into the prepared jars, leaving ½ inch of headspace. Use a nonmetallic utensil to release any air bubbles. Wipe the rims clean and seal with the lids and rings.

Continued

CLASSIC TOMATO SAUCE WITH VARIATIONS

CONTINUED

6. Process in a hot water bath (see page 31): 35 minutes for pint jars, or 40 minutes for quart jars. Turn off the heat and let the jars rest in the water bath for 10 minutes.

7. Carefully remove the jars from the hot water canner. Set aside to cool for 12 hours.

8. Check the lids for proper seals (see page 32). Remove the rings, wipe the jars, label and date them, and transfer to a cupboard or pantry.

9. Refrigerate any jars that don't seal properly, and use within 5 days. Properly sealed jars will last in the cupboard for 12 months. Once opened, refrigerate and consume within 5 days.

TRY INSTEAD

Just because this recipe excludes seasoning and additional flavors doesn't mean you have to. Adding several sprigs of fresh basil, thyme, or oregano is great, as long as the flavors are a good match for the way you cook.

CLASSIC MARINARA SAUCE

MAKES 4 PINT JARS

WATER-BATH CANNING

This simple, yet versatile, sauce can be used to make a traditional spaghetti dinner as well as many other tomato-based meals. Measure the ingredients. Do not be tempted to add additional onions or garlic, as the ratio in this recipe must be maintained to ensure safety.

PREP TIME: 35 minutes
COOK TIME: 1 hour
PROCESSING TIME: 35 minutes
TOTAL TIME: 2 hours, 10 minutes

9 pounds Roma or other paste tomatoes, chopped
1 cup chopped onion
3 garlic cloves, chopped
1 bay leaf
1 teaspoon salt
1 teaspoon dried oregano
1 teaspoon sugar (optional)
4 tablespoons bottled lemon juice, divided

1. Prepare a hot water bath (see page 30). Place the jars in it to keep warm. Wash the lids and rings in hot, soapy water, and set aside.

2. In a large pot set over a high heat, combine the tomatoes and onion. Bring to a boil. Reduce the heat to maintain a low boil, stirring regularly for about 20 minutes. Break up the tomatoes with a spoon or potato masher as they soften.

3. Add the garlic, bay leaf, salt, oregano, and sugar (if using). Reduce the heat to medium. Simmer for about 40 minutes, or until the sauce is reduced by nearly one-half.

4. Using a food mill, run the sauce through to remove the seeds, skins, and bay leaf. Discard these. Return the sauce to the pot and bring back to a rolling boil.

5. Fill each jar with 1 tablespoon of lemon juice.

6. Ladle the hot sauce into the prepared jars, leaving ½ inch of headspace. Use a nonmetallic utensil to release any air bubbles. Wipe the rims clean and seal with the lids and rings.

7. Process the jars in a hot water bath (see page 31) for 35 minutes. Turn off the heat and let the jars rest in the water bath for 10 minutes.

Continued

CLASSIC MARINARA SAUCE

CONTINUED

8. Carefully remove the jars from the hot water canner. Set aside to cool for 12 hours.

9. Check the lids for proper seals (see page 32). Remove the rings, wipe the jars, label and date them, and transfer to a cupboard or pantry.

10. Refrigerate any jars that don't seal properly, and use within 3 weeks. Properly sealed jars will last in the cupboard for 12 months. Once opened, refrigerate and consume within 3 weeks.

PREPARATION TIP

It is important to follow the directions for reheating this sauce after running it through the food mill. Failure to reheat the sauce can result in spoilage microorganisms and/or sealing failure. For the best product, and to get a good seal on the jars, pack the jars one at a time from start to finish, placing them into the canner as you go, instead of packing them all at once.

PIZZA SAUCE

MAKES 4 PINT JARS

WATER-BATH CANNING

Putting up tomatoes is a labor of love that reaps its rewards when you reach in your pantry throughout the year. Skip the overly sweetened and high-sodium pizza sauces and whip up a batch of this winner—you may never order pizza again. Double, triple, or quadruple the recipe, depending on how often your family eats pizza, and be stocked up all year. One pint jar typically covers 2 large pizzas.

PREP TIME: 40 minutes, plus 20 minutes draining time
COOK TIME: 35 minutes
PROCESSING TIME: 35 minutes
TOTAL TIME: 2 hours, 10 minutes

10 pounds Roma or other paste tomatoes, peeled, quartered, cored, and seeded.
½ cup bottled lemon juice
1 teaspoon dried oregano
1 teaspoon dried parsley
1 teaspoon salt
1 teaspoon freshly ground black pepper
1 teaspoon garlic powder
1 teaspoon onion powder

1. In a colander, drain the tomatoes for 20 minutes. Discard the liquid.

2. Prepare a hot water bath (see page 30). Place the jars in it to keep warm. Wash the lids and rings in hot, soapy water, and set aside.

3. In a food processor, purée the tomatoes in batches. Measure 13 cups of purée and add to a large pot. Reserve any extra for another use.

4. Bring the purée to a full, rolling boil over medium-high heat, stirring occasionally.

5. Add the lemon juice, oregano, parsley, salt, pepper, garlic powder, and onion powder. Continue to boil hard for 20 to 30 minutes, or until the sauce has thickened just slightly. Remove from the heat.

6. Ladle the hot pizza sauce into the prepared jars, leaving ½ inch of headspace. Use a nonmetallic utensil to release any air bubbles. Wipe the rims clean and seal with the lids and rings.

7. Process the jars in a hot water bath (see page 31) for 35 minutes. Turn off the heat and let the jars rest in the water bath for 10 minutes.

8. Carefully remove the jars from the hot water canner. Set aside to cool for 12 hours.

Continued

PIZZA SAUCE

CONTINUED

9. Check the lids for proper seals (see page 32). Remove the rings, wipe the jars, label and date them, and transfer to a cupboard or pantry.

10. Refrigerate any jars that don't seal properly, and use within 3 weeks. Properly sealed jars will last in the cupboard for 12 months. Once opened, refrigerate and consume within 3 weeks.

LOW-SODIUM PREPARATION TIP

To decrease the sodium, simply omit or decrease the amount of salt. Because this recipe has plenty of spices in it, the sauce will not suffer and will still taste great with your favorite pizza toppings.

HOUSE-STYLE HOT SAUCE

MAKES 7 HALF-PINT JARS

WATER-BATH CANNING

Making your own house-style hot sauce lets you adjust the heat, texture, and flavor so you have it just the way you like it. For a chunky texture, this sauce is ready to pack and process right out of the pot. If you prefer a smoother sauce, strain it before packing it into jars. Any variety of hot chiles can be substituted for the serranos—use whatever is ripe and satisfies your personal heat tolerance. Tomatoes add body. If you prefer a relish consisting solely of hot chiles, you'll likely enjoy Sandwich Relish (see page 140), too.

PREP TIME: 15 minutes
COOK TIME: 30 minutes
PROCESSING TIME: 10 minutes
TOTAL TIME: 55 minutes

- 4 pounds (about 12) tomatoes, stemmed and chopped
- ½ cup chopped serrano peppers
- 4 cups white vinegar
- 2 teaspoons salt

1. Prepare a hot water bath (see page 30). Place the jars in it to keep warm. Wash the lids and rings in hot, soapy water, and set aside.

2. To a large saucepot set over medium heat (you may need two pots), add the tomatoes in batches, crushing with a potato masher or a wooden spoon until all are incorporated. Bring to a simmer. Cook for about 5 minutes, stirring frequently, or until the tomatoes are soft.

3. Add the serrano peppers. Simmer for 15 to 20 minutes, or until tender.

4. In a food processor or blender, purée the mixture until smooth. Strain through a fine sieve into a clean saucepot. Use a spatula to press out as much juice as possible. Discard the remaining pulp.

5. Bring the pot to a simmer over medium heat. Add the vinegar and salt. Continue to simmer for 5 minutes more.

6. Ladle the hot sauce into the prepared jars, leaving ½ inch of headspace. Use a nonmetallic utensil to release any air bubbles. Wipe the rims clean and seal with the lids and rings.

7. Process the jars in a hot water bath (see page 31) for 10 minutes. Turn off the heat and let the jars rest in the water bath for 10 minutes.

8. Carefully remove the jars from the hot water canner. Set aside to cool for 12 hours.

Continued

HOUSE-STYLE HOT SAUCE

CONTINUED

9. Check the lids for proper seals (see page 32). Remove the rings, wipe the jars, label and date them, and transfer to a cupboard or pantry.

10. Refrigerate any jars that don't seal properly, and use within 2 months. Properly sealed jars will last in the cupboard for 12 months. Once opened, refrigerate and consume within 2 months.

LOW-SODIUM PREPARATION TIP

The salt in this recipe can be safely omitted or reduced. Try using just ½ to 1 teaspoon of canning salt and see what you think. If it tastes good to you with this lower amount of salt, leave it as is and proceed with the recipe. If not, add a bit more until the sauce is seasoned to your liking.

MOSTARDO (PEAR MUSTARD)

MAKES 4 PINT JARS

WATER-BATH CANNING, LOW-SODIUM

This hot and spicy preserve comes from Italy where it is served with cured sausages and meats, cheeses, and other relishes. Using overripe fruit will produce the richest flavor. The fruit is added in stages, the firmest fruits first and the most tender last, so the finished sauce has the right consistency.

PREP TIME: 30 minutes
COOK TIME: 45 minutes
PROCESSING TIME: 10 minutes
TOTAL TIME: 1 hour, 25 minutes

- 3½ cups sugar
- 2 cups white wine vinegar
- 3 tablespoons mustard seed
- 1 pound pears, cored, stemmed, and thinly sliced (about 2 cups)
- 8 ounces quince, cored, stemmed, and thinly sliced (about 1 cup)
- 10 ounces fresh figs, stemmed and quartered (about 2 cups)
- 8 ounces peaches, peeled, pitted, and thinly sliced (about 1 cup)
- 8 ounces apricots, pitted and quartered (about 1 cup)
- 8 ounces sweet or sour cherries, pitted (about 1½ cups)

1. Prepare a hot water bath (see page 30). Place the jars in it to keep warm. Wash the lids and rings in hot, soapy water, and set aside.

2. In a preserving pot or a deep pot set over high heat, combine the sugar, vinegar, and mustard seed. Bring to a boil, stirring to dissolve the sugar. Reduce the heat to medium.

3. Add the pears and quince. Simmer for 10 minutes.

4. Add the figs, peaches, and apricots. Simmer for another 10 minutes.

5. Add the cherries. Simmer for 15 to 20 minutes more, or until very tender and the syrup is thick.

6. Ladle the hot *mostardo* into the prepared jars, leaving ¼ inch of headspace. Use a nonmetallic utensil to release any air bubbles. Wipe the rims clean and seal with the lids and rings.

7. Process the jars in a hot water bath (see page 31) for 10 minutes. Turn off the heat and let the jars rest in the water bath for 10 minutes.

8. Carefully remove the jars from the hot water canner. Set aside to cool for 12 hours.

9. Check the lids for proper seals (see page 32). Remove the rings, wipe the jars, label and date them, and transfer to a cupboard or pantry.

10. Refrigerate any jars that don't seal properly, and use within 6 weeks. Properly sealed jars will last in the cupboard for 12 months. Once opened, refrigerate and consume within 6 weeks.

BLUEBERRY KETCHUP

MAKES 3 HALF-PINT JARS

WATER-BATH CANNING, LOW-SODIUM

You have options galore here. This ketchup is a great condiment for grilled fish and seafood. It is also a perfect addition to glazes and marinades for chicken and pork. You can make a flavorful vinaigrette by blending this with a nut oil or extra-virgin olive oil.

PREP TIME: 5 minutes
COOK TIME: 15 minutes
PROCESSING TIME: 15 minutes
TOTAL TIME: 35 minutes

2 cups fresh or frozen blueberries
⅓ cup apple cider vinegar
2 tablespoons balsamic vinegar
Juice of 1 lime
¾ cup firmly packed brown sugar
1 teaspoon ground cinnamon
½ teaspoon ground cloves
½ teaspoon ground ginger
½ teaspoon salt
¼ teaspoon cayenne pepper

1. Prepare a hot water bath (see page 30). Place the jars in it to keep warm. Wash the lids and rings in hot, soapy water, and set aside.

2. In a medium saucepan set over high heat, combine the blueberries, cider vinegar, balsamic vinegar, and lime juice. Bring to a boil. Reduce the heat to medium. Simmer for 5 minutes. Strain the blueberry mixture through a sieve into a clean saucepan, pressing with a rubber spatula or wooden spoon to extract as much pulp as possible. Discard the seeds.

3. Add the brown sugar, cinnamon, cloves, ginger, salt, and cayenne pepper to the blueberry mixture. Bring to a full rolling boil over high heat, stirring to dissolve the sugar. Reduce the heat to medium. Simmer for about 10 minutes more, or until thickened.

4. Ladle the hot blueberry ketchup into the prepared jars, leaving ¼ inch of headspace. Use a nonmetallic utensil to release any air bubbles. Wipe the rims clean and seal with the lids and rings.

5. Process the jars in a hot water bath (see page 31) for 15 minutes. Turn off the heat and let the jars rest in the water bath for 10 minutes.

6. Carefully remove the jars from the hot water canner. Set aside to cool for 12 hours.

7. Check the lids for proper seals (see page 32). Remove the rings, wipe the jars, label and date them, and transfer to a cupboard or pantry.

8. Refrigerate any jars that don't seal properly, and use within 3 weeks. Properly sealed jars will last in the cupboard for 12 months. Once opened, refrigerate and consume within 3 weeks.

TRY INSTEAD

To add additional flavor to this ketchup, add a few fresh rosemary or thyme sprigs to the blueberries while you simmer them in the water and lime juice. Remove and discard the herb sprigs before puréeing the berries.

TOMATO KETCHUP

MAKES 4 HALF-PINT JARS

WATER-BATH CANNING

Once upon a time, ketchup was not the cloyingly sweet condiment we know today but instead, a homemade delight with lots of character. This ketchup delivers on flavor, while still being significantly lower in sugar than store-bought versions. Spread it on a burger or dip some fries in it. If you are adventurous, further customize it to suit your taste.

PREP TIME: 25 minutes
COOK TIME: 2 hours
PROCESSING TIME: 10 minutes
TOTAL TIME: 2 hours, 35 minutes

7 pounds Roma or other paste tomatoes
1 large onion, chopped
1 cup apple cider vinegar
½ cup firmly packed brown sugar
2 teaspoons kosher salt
¼ teaspoon cayenne pepper
1 teaspoon mustard seed
1 teaspoon whole cloves
1 teaspoon whole allspice berries
1 cinnamon stick, broken

1. In a large pot set over high heat, combine the tomatoes and onion. Bring the mixture to a boil. Reduce the heat to low. Simmer for 30 minutes, or until very soft.

2. Using a food mill, pass the mixture through to purée. Discard the seeds and skins. Rinse the pot, place it on the stove, and return the purée to it.

3. Prepare a hot water bath (see page 30). Place the jars in it to keep warm. Wash the lids and rings in hot, soapy water, and set aside.

4. Add the cider vinegar, brown sugar, kosher salt, and cayenne pepper to the purée.

LOW-SUGAR PREPARATION TIP

This recipe is already low in sugar compared to supermarket brands; however it is possible to omit all processed sugar. If you opt for this, add a couple pieces of fresh fruit, such as two or three chopped nectarines or plums, instead, in the first step along with the tomatoes for a little more natural sweetness.

5. In a cheesecloth square, combine the mustard seed, cloves, allspice, and cinnamon. Tie securely with kitchen twine into a sachet. Add to the pot. Simmer over low heat for about 1 hour, 30 minutes, or until reduced by half. Remove and discard the sachet.

6. Ladle the hot ketchup into the prepared jars, leaving ½ inch of headspace. Use a nonmetallic utensil to release any air bubbles. Wipe the rims clean and seal with the lids and rings.

7. Process the jars in a hot water bath (see page 31) for 10 minutes. Turn off the heat and let the jars rest in the water bath for 10 minutes.

8. Carefully remove the jars from the hot water canner. Set aside to cool for 12 hours.

9. Check the lids for proper seals (see page 32). Remove the rings, wipe the jars, label and date them, and transfer to a cupboard or pantry.

10. Refrigerate any jars that don't seal properly, and use within 4 weeks. Properly sealed jars will last in the cupboard for 12 months. Once opened, refrigerate and consume within 4 weeks.

LOW-SODIUM PREPARATION TIP

Cut out the salt totally or simply reduce the amount to 1 teaspoon or less, as desired. When lowering the salt, you may want to increase the amount of other seasonings, such as the cayenne pepper or mustard seed, to increase the flavor and allow it to stand on its own and still taste great—even without the salt.

TOMATO PASTE

MAKES 8 QUARTER-PINT JARS

WATER-BATH CANNING, LOW-SODIUM

This infinitely versatile product is used in so many ways that you will be thrilled to have a steady supply in your cupboards. More flavorful than commercial varieties, the thickened tomato paste is best made from tomatoes at the height of ripeness. Using quarter-pint jars is a great way to minimize waste, as most recipes typically call for only a tablespoon or two. This recipe requires time, so plan ahead to get it done in a day.

PREP TIME: 30 minutes
COOK TIME: 8 hours, 30 minutes
PROCESSING TIME: 45 minutes
TOTAL TIME: 9 hours, 45 minutes

3 gallons quartered Roma or other paste tomatoes
1 red bell pepper, seeded and chopped
1 bay leaf
½ teaspoon kosher salt
6 teaspoons bottled lemon juice, divided

1. In a large pot set over high heat, combine the tomatoes, red bell pepper, bay leaf, and salt. Bring to a boil. Reduce the heat to low. Simmer for 30 minutes, or until the tomatoes are very soft. Using a potato masher, press the tomatoes down and release their juices while they are cooking.

2. Using a food mill, pass the mixture through to purée. Discard the seeds and skins. Transfer the purée to an uncovered slow cooker set on low.

3. Cook the tomatoes for 8 hours, stirring hourly. As it thickens and reduces, check more frequently to prevent scorching.

4. Prepare a hot water bath (see page 30). Place the jars in it to keep warm. Wash the lids and rings in hot, soapy water, and set aside.

5. To each jar, add ¾ teaspoon of lemon juice.

6. Ladle the hot paste into the prepared jars, leaving ½ inch of headspace. Use a nonmetallic utensil to release any air bubbles. Wipe the rims clean and seal with the lids and rings.

7. Process the jars in a hot water bath (see page 31) for 45 minutes. Turn off the heat and let the jars rest in the water bath for 10 minutes.

8. Carefully remove the jars from the hot water canner. Set aside to cool for 12 hours.

9. Check the lids for proper seals (see page 32). Remove the rings, wipe the jars, label and date them, and transfer to a cupboard or pantry.

10. Refrigerate any jars that don't seal properly, and use within 3 weeks. Properly sealed jars will last in the cupboard for 12 months. Once opened, refrigerate and consume within 3 weeks.

PREPARATION TIP

You can make this recipe without a food mill, though it will take more time. Bring a large pot of water to a boil, and prepare an ice bath in the sink or a large bowl. Cut a small "X" into the skin of each tomato. Blanch the tomatoes in the boiling water, in batches, for 1 to 2 minutes, or until their skins begin to curl. With a slotted spoon, immediately transfer them to the ice bath to stop the cooking. Once cool, slip off the skins. Cut the tomatoes into quarters, removing the seeds with your fingers as you go. Drain in a colander for a few minutes, purée in a blender or food processor, and proceed with the recipe from Step 3.

6

SALSAS, RELISHES & CHUTNEYS

The flavors may be complex, but in reality, salsas, relishes, and chutneys are quite simple to make at home. The diverse mix of offerings in this chapter is just what you need to take simple meals to extraordinary. Whether you like spicy, sweet, or a combination of the two, there are plenty of projects in this chapter that can effortlessly liven up your mealtime.

SALSA VERDE

MAKES 4 PINT JARS

WATER-BATH CANNING, SEASONAL, LOW-SODIUM

Tomatillos are increasingly easy to find in most markets. Many gardeners love to include them in their plots for the plant's beauty and pleasant scent. Their high-producing characteristics are an added bonus. Serve this as part of a salsa smorgasbord with tortilla chips or spoon it over tacos, enchiladas, or bean stews and soups.

PREP TIME: 20 minutes
COOK TIME: 10 minutes
PROCESSING TIME: 15 minutes
TOTAL TIME: 45 minutes

- 2 pounds tomatillos, husks removed and coarsely chopped (about 6 cups)
- 1 cup chopped onion
- 1 cup chopped green chiles
- 4 garlic cloves, minced
- 2 tablespoons minced fresh cilantro
- 2 teaspoons ground cumin
- ½ teaspoon salt
- ½ teaspoon red pepper flakes
- ½ cup white vinegar
- ¼ cup freshly squeezed lime juice

1. Prepare a hot water bath (see page 30). Place the jars in it to keep warm. Wash the lids and rings in hot, soapy water, and set aside.

2. In a preserving pot or saucepot set over medium-high heat, combine the tomatillos, onion, chiles, garlic, cilantro, cumin, salt, and red pepper flakes.

3. Add the white vinegar and lime juice. Bring to a boil. Boil for 10 minutes.

4. Ladle the salsa into the prepared jars, leaving ½ inch of headspace. Use a nonmetallic utensil to release any air bubbles. Wipe the rims clean and seal with the lids and rings.

5. Process the jars in a hot water bath (see page 31) for 15 minutes. Turn off the heat and let the jars rest in the water bath for 10 minutes.

6. Carefully remove the jars from the hot water canner. Set aside to cool for 12 hours.

7. Check the lids for proper seals (see page 32). Remove the rings, wipe the jars, label and date them, and transfer to a cupboard or pantry.

8. Refrigerate any jars that don't seal properly, and use within 2 months. Properly sealed jars will last in the cupboard for 12 months. Once opened, refrigerate and consume within 2 months.

PARTY SALSA

MAKES 3 PINT JARS

WATER-BATH CANNING

Letting the salsa ferment adds a subtle richness to this popular relish. Look beyond the tortilla chips, and serve this salsa as a topping for fish or chicken, chili (con carne or not), enchiladas, and burritos—even eggs. Use a variety of tomatoes for a nuanced flavor.

PREP TIME: 20 minutes
COOK TIME: 10 minutes
PROCESSING TIME: 15 minutes
TOTAL TIME: 45 minutes

6 cups peeled, seeded, and diced tomatoes
2 small yellow onions, chopped fine
2 jalapeño peppers, seeded and chopped
1 bunch fresh cilantro, chopped
½ cup white vinegar
¼ cup freshly squeezed lime juice
1 tablespoon sea salt
6 garlic cloves
1 teaspoon dried oregano

1. Prepare a hot water bath (see page 30). Place the jars in it to keep warm. Wash the lids and rings in hot, soapy water, and set aside.

2. In a preserving pot or saucepot set over medium-high heat, stir together the tomatoes, onions, jalapeños, cilantro, white vinegar, lime juice, sea salt, garlic, and oregano. Bring to a boil. Cook for 10 minutes.

3. Ladle the salsa into the prepared jars, leaving ½ inch of headspace. Use a nonmetallic utensil to release any air bubbles. Wipe the rims clean and seal with the lids and rings.

4. Process the jars in a hot water bath (see page 31) for 15 minutes. Turn off the heat and let the jars rest in the water bath for 10 minutes.

5. Carefully remove the jars from the hot water canner. Set aside to cool for 12 hours.

6. Check the lids for proper seals (see page 32). Remove the rings, wipe the jars, label and date them, and transfer to a cupboard or pantry.

7. Refrigerate any jars that don't seal properly, and use within 1 month. Properly sealed jars will last in the cupboard for 12 months. Once opened, refrigerate and consume within 1 month.

SPICY TOMATO SALSA

MAKES 3 PINT JARS

WATER-BATH CANNING

When you want a simple salsa, this will be your go-to recipe. It does not have all the bells and whistles of more traditional salsas, but delivers a spicy tomato punch that works as well on a chip as a burrito, enchilada, or taco. Be sure to use Roma tomatoes, as their thin skins need no peeling, and their low moisture content creates a thick and chunky texture.

6

SALSAS, RELISHES & CHUTNEYS

PREP TIME: 25 minutes
COOK TIME: 10 minutes
PROCESSING TIME: 15 minutes
TOTAL TIME: 50 minutes

6 cups cored and diced Roma tomatoes
2 cups diced jalapeño peppers
2 cups diced green bell peppers
1 cup diced red onion
½ cup bottled lime juice
1½ teaspoons pickling salt

1. Prepare a hot water bath (see page 30). Place the jars in it to keep warm. Wash the lids and rings in hot, soapy water, and set aside.

2. In a large saucepot set over medium-high heat, combine the tomatoes, jalapeños, green bell peppers, onion, lime juice, and pickling salt. Bring to a boil. Reduce the heat to low. Simmer for 10 minutes, stirring occasionally.

3. Ladle the salsa into the prepared jars, leaving ½ inch of headspace. Use a nonmetallic utensil to release any air bubbles. Wipe the rims clean and seal with the lids and rings.

4. Process the jars in a hot water bath (see page 31) for 15 minutes. Turn off the heat and let the jars rest in the water bath for 10 minutes.

5. Carefully remove the jars from the hot water canner. Set aside to cool for 12 hours.

6. Check the lids for proper seals (see page 32). Remove the rings, wipe the jars, label and date them, and transfer to a cupboard or pantry.

7. Refrigerate any jars that don't seal properly, and use within 1 month. Properly sealed jars will last in the cupboard for 12 months. Once opened, refrigerate and consume within 1 month.

PEACH-APRICOT SALSA

MAKES 4 HALF-PINT JARS

WATER-BATH CANNING, LOW-SODIUM

Fruit lovers are smitten with this sweet and spicy salsa that combines some of the best flavors of summer. Eat it with tortilla chips, spoon it over pancakes or waffles, or fill crepes with this unique and flavor-packed delight. To prevent the peaches in this recipe from browning, put the vinegar in a medium saucepot and add the peaches immediately after they've been peeled and chopped.

PREP TIME: 20 minutes
COOK TIME: 5 minutes
PROCESSING TIME: 15 minutes
TOTAL TIME: 40 minutes

¼ cup white vinegar (see above)
2½ cups peeled and chopped peaches
½ cup peeled, pitted, and chopped apricots
¾ cup diced red onion
1 jalapeño pepper, seeded and chopped
1 garlic clove, chopped
½ red bell pepper, chopped
¼ cup fresh cilantro, finely chopped
1 teaspoon ground cumin
¼ to ½ teaspoon cayenne pepper
1 tablespoon honey

1. Prepare a hot water bath (see page 30). Place the jars in it to keep warm. Wash the lids and rings in hot, soapy water, and set aside.

2. Place the saucepot with the peaches and vinegar over medium-high heat. Add the apricots, red onion, jalapeño, garlic, red bell pepper, cilantro, cumin, cayenne pepper, and honey. Stir to combine. Bring to a boil. Cook for about 5 minutes, stirring frequently, or until the salsa begins to thicken slightly.

3. Ladle the salsa into the prepared jars, leaving ½ inch of headspace. Use a nonmetallic utensil to release any air bubbles. Wipe the rims clean and seal with the lids and rings.

4. Process the jars in a hot water bath (see page 31) for 15 minutes. Turn off the heat and let the jars rest in the water bath for 10 minutes.

5. Carefully remove the jars from the hot water canner. Set aside to cool for 12 hours.

6. Check the lids for proper seals (see page 32). Remove the rings, wipe the jars, label and date them, and transfer to a cupboard or pantry.

7. Refrigerate any jars that don't seal properly, and use within 2 months. Properly sealed jars will last in the cupboard for 12 months. Once opened, refrigerate and consume within 2 months.

PICCALILLI

MAKES 6 HALF-PINT JARS

WATER-BATH CANNING

"Piccalilli"—a classic pickle cherished by the British—is also known as India relish or chowchow. It is a classic ingredient in a dish called Ploughman's Lunch, composed of bread, cheese, cold meat, and pickles. Serve this slightly sweet relish with pâtés, sausages, or eggs.

PREP TIME: 25 minutes,
plus 12 hours fermentation time
COOK TIME: 20 minutes
PROCESSING TIME: 10 minutes
TOTAL TIME: 12 hours, 55 minutes

- 1½ heads cabbage, chopped (about 5 cups)
- 4 cups chopped green tomatoes
- 1½ cups chopped onion
- 3 tablespoons salt
- ¼ cup pickling spices
- 4 tablespoons chopped fresh ginger
- 2 tablespoons yellow mustard seed
- 3 cups white vinegar
- 1¾ cups water
- 1 cup sugar
- 2 teaspoons ground turmeric

DAY 1

1. In a large container or crock, mix together the cabbage, green tomatoes, and onion. Knead with your hands for about 10 minutes, or until the cabbage releases some of its juices.

2. Add the salt and toss to mix evenly.

3. Put a plate on top of the vegetables, and add enough weight so they are relatively compact. Ferment at room temperature for 12 hours.

DAY 2

1. Prepare a hot water bath (see page 30). Place the jars in it to keep warm. Wash the lids and rings in hot, soapy water, and set aside.

2. Drain the vegetables and, if available, use a salad spinner to remove as much moisture as possible.

3. In a cheesecloth square, combine the pickling spices, ginger, and mustard seed. Tie securely with kitchen twine into a sachet.

4. In a large saucepan set over medium-high heat, combine the vinegar, water, sugar, turmeric, and the sachet. Bring to a boil.

5. Add the drained vegetables. Cook for about 20 minutes, or until thickened. Remove and discard the sachet.

6. Ladle the piccalilli into the prepared jars, leaving ½ inch of headspace. Use a nonmetallic utensil to release any air bubbles. Wipe the rims clean and seal with the lids and rings.

7. Process the jars in a hot water bath (see page 31) for 10 minutes. Turn off the heat and let the jars rest in the water bath for 10 minutes.

8. Carefully remove the jars from the hot water canner. Set aside to cool for 12 hours.

9. Check the lids for proper seals (see page 32). Remove the rings, wipe the jars, label and date them, and transfer to a cupboard or pantry.

10. Let the piccalilli rest for at least 3 weeks before serving. Refrigerate any jars that don't seal properly, and use within 2 months. Properly sealed jars will last in the cupboard for 12 months. Once opened, refrigerate and consume within 2 months.

SANDWICH RELISH

MAKES 4 PINT JARS

WATER-BATH CANNING

No matter what you call your sandwiches—hoagies, submarines, heroes, or Dagwoods—this spicy relish is the perfect finish. It's also a crowd favorite topping hamburgers and hot dogs. Alter the ratio of sweet and hot peppers to hit the right note for your crowd. For a milder relish, replace some of the chiles with sweet bell peppers.

PREP TIME: 20 minutes, plus 10 minutes resting time
COOK TIME: 20 minutes
PROCESSING TIME: 15 minutes
TOTAL TIME: 1 hour, 5 minutes

20 red chiles, stemmed, halved, seeded, and coarsely chopped
10 green chiles, stemmed, halved, seeded, and coarsely chopped
1 tablespoon canning salt
2 pounds onions, peeled and chopped
1 ½ cups apple cider vinegar
1 ½ cups sugar

1. Prepare a hot water bath (see page 30). Place the jars in it to keep warm. Wash the lids and rings in hot, soapy water, and set aside.

2. In a food processor, process the chiles into a coarse paste. Transfer to a bowl. Add the canning salt and enough boiling water to cover. Let stand for 10 minutes. Drain.

3. In a preserving pot or saucepot set over medium-high heat, mix together the ground chiles and onions. Add the vinegar and sugar. Bring to a boil. Boil for 20 minutes.

4. Ladle the relish into the prepared jars, leaving ½ inch of headspace. Use a nonmetallic utensil to release any air bubbles. Wipe the rims clean and seal with the lids and rings.

5. Process the jars in a hot water bath (see page 31) for 15 minutes. Turn off the heat and let the jars rest in the water bath for 10 minutes.

6. Carefully remove the jars from the hot water canner. Set aside to cool for 12 hours.

7. Check the lids for proper seals (see page 32). Remove the rings, wipe the jars, label and date them, and transfer to a cupboard or pantry.

8. Refrigerate any jars that don't seal properly, and use within 1 month. Properly sealed jars will last in the cupboard for 12 months. Once opened, refrigerate and consume within 1 month.

PREPARATION TIP

When preparing a large amount of hot peppers, it is important to cover your hands with kitchen gloves to prevent burns. While you may not notice any effect when cutting one or two peppers, a large amount can cause significant irritation. Also, do not touch your eyes or nose while working with these peppers and wash your hands thoroughly when finished.

CUCUMBER RELISH

MAKES 4 HALF-PINT JARS

WATER-BATH CANNING

This mild, slightly sweet relish goes well on a hot dog, hamburger, or alongside other barbecued meats. To prevent ending up with a runny relish, plan for the extra resting time so the vegetables release plenty of water before you begin the cooking.

PREP TIME: 15 minutes, plus 4 hours resting time
COOK TIME: 10 minutes
PROCESSING TIME: 10 minutes
TOTAL TIME: 4 hours, 35 minutes

3 cups diced pickling cucumbers
¾ cup finely chopped red bell pepper
¾ cup finely chopped green bell pepper
1 celery stalk, finely chopped
1 jalapeño pepper, finely chopped
3 tablespoons pickling salt
1½ cups white vinegar
⅓ cup sugar
1 tablespoon chopped garlic
¾ teaspoon dried thyme

1. In a large bowl, combine the cucumbers, red bell pepper, green bell pepper, celery, jalapeño, and pickling salt. Cover with a clean kitchen towel. Let stand at room temperature for 4 hours. Drain in a colander and rinse thoroughly.

2. Prepare a hot water bath (see page 30). Place the jars in it to keep warm. Wash the lids and rings in hot, soapy water, and set aside.

3. In a large saucepot set over medium-high heat, combine the white vinegar and sugar. Bring to a boil, stirring until the sugar dissolves.

4. Add the drained vegetables, garlic, and thyme. Return the mixture to a boil.

5. Ladle the relish into the prepared jars, leaving ½ inch of headspace. Use a nonmetallic utensil to release any air bubbles. Wipe the rims clean and seal with the lids and rings.

6. Process the jars in a hot water bath (see page 31) for 10 minutes. Turn off the heat and let the jars rest in the water bath for 10 minutes.

7. Carefully remove the jars from the hot water canner. Set aside to cool for 12 hours.

8. Check the lids for proper seals (see page 32). Remove the rings, wipe the jars, label and date them, and transfer to a cupboard or pantry.

9. Refrigerate any jars that don't seal properly, and use within 2 months. Properly sealed jars will last in the cupboard for 12 months. Once opened, refrigerate and consume within 2 months.

CLOSER LOOK

Use pickling cucumbers for pickle recipes. With a thicker skin, a more bitter taste, and smaller seeds, these pickles are specifically grown for pickling. While some grocery stores carry pickling cucumbers, they are most often found at produce and farmers' markets at the height of summer. For best results, use cucumbers within a day or two of picking.

ZUCCHINI RELISH

MAKES 4 PINT JARS

WATER-BATH CANNING

If you've ever grown your own zucchini, you (and your friends and neighbors) know how prolific this summer squash can be. While welcomed with joy early in the summer, by the end, finding ways to use the massive green squash can become a bit cumbersome. This spicy relish will use up one medium squash. If you double or triple the recipe, you will have plenty to give as gifts.

PREP TIME: 15 minutes, plus 12 hours resting time
COOK TIME: 15 minutes
PROCESSING TIME: 10 minutes
TOTAL TIME: 12 hours, 40 minutes

4 cups finely diced zucchini
2 cups finely chopped red and/or green bell peppers
1 cup finely chopped onion
2 tablespoons pickling salt
2 cups white vinegar
1 cup sugar
2 tablespoons prepared horseradish
1 teaspoon mustard seed

DAY 1

1. In a large bowl, combine the zucchini, bell peppers, onion, and pickling salt.

2. Cover with a clean kitchen towel. Let stand at room temperature for 12 hours, or overnight.

DAY 2

1. Drain the vegetables in a colander and rinse thoroughly. With clean hands, squeeze out any excess water.

2. Prepare a hot water bath (see page 30). Place the jars in it to keep warm. Wash the lids and rings in hot, soapy water, and set aside.

3. In a medium saucepot set over medium-high heat, combine the white vinegar, sugar, horseradish, and mustard seed. Bring to a boil, stirring until the sugar dissolves.

4. Add the drained vegetables. Return the mixture to a boil. Reduce the heat to low. Simmer for 10 minutes.

5. Ladle the relish into the prepared jars, leaving ¼ inch of headspace. Use a nonmetallic utensil to release any air bubbles. Wipe the rims clean and seal with the lids and rings.

6. Process the jars in a hot water bath (see page 31) for 10 minutes. Turn off the heat and let the jars rest in the water bath for 10 minutes.

7. Carefully remove the jars from the hot water canner. Set aside to cool for 12 hours.

8. Check the lids for proper seals (see page 32). Remove the rings, wipe the jars, label and date them, and transfer to a cupboard or pantry.

9. Refrigerate any jars that don't seal properly, and use within 2 months. Properly sealed jars will last in the cupboard for 12 months. Once opened, refrigerate and consume within 2 months.

PREPARATION TIP

To reduce the chopping time, use a meat grinder to process the zucchini, peppers, and onions. This will create an almost creamy, spreadable relish.

PEACH CHUTNEY

MAKES 5 PINT JARS

WATER-BATH CANNING, LOW-SODIUM

Garam masala is a classic Indian spice mixture that adds the flavors of cardamom, cumin, cloves, nutmeg, cinnamon, and star anise to this chutney. Reserve any lower-quality peaches or a bushel of seconds for a batch of chutney. Just trim away any bruises or brown spots. Don't use fruits, though, with moldy spots—toss those out.

PREP TIME: 25 minutes
COOK TIME: 1 hour
PROCESSING TIME: 10 minutes
TOTAL TIME: 1 hour, 35 minutes

5 pounds yellow peaches, or nectarines, peeled, pitted, and cut into ½-inch dice
2 cups sugar
1½ cups apple cider vinegar
1 cup chopped sweet onion
¾ cup raisins
2 or 3 jalapeño peppers, diced
1 sweet banana pepper, or ½ yellow bell pepper, diced
3 tablespoons mustard seed
2 tablespoons grated fresh ginger
2 garlic cloves, minced
1 teaspoon garam masala
½ teaspoon ground turmeric

1. Prepare a hot water bath (see page 30). Place the jars in it to keep warm. Wash the lids and rings in hot, soapy water, and set aside.

2. In a deep pot or a preserving pot set over medium heat, combine the peaches, sugar, cider vinegar, onion, raisins, jalapeños, banana pepper, mustard seed, ginger, garlic, garam masala, and turmeric. Slowly bring to a boil, stirring frequently. Reduce the heat to low. Simmer for 1 hour, or until very thick.

3. Ladle the chutney into the prepared jars, leaving ¼ inch of headspace. Use a nonmetallic utensil to release any air bubbles. Wipe the rims clean and seal with the lids and rings.

4. Process the jars in a hot water bath (see page 31) for 10 minutes. Turn off the heat and let the jars rest in the water bath for 10 minutes.

5. Carefully remove the jars from the hot water canner. Set aside to cool for 12 hours.

6. Check the lids for proper seals (see page 32). Remove the rings, wipe the jars, label and date them, and transfer to a cupboard or pantry.

7. For the best flavor, allow the chutney to cure for 3 to 4 weeks before serving. Refrigerate any jars that don't seal properly, and use within 6 weeks. Properly sealed jars will last in the cupboard for 12 months. Once opened, refrigerate and consume within 6 weeks.

GINGER-LIME CHUTNEY

MAKES 2 PINT JARS

WATER-BATH CANNING, LOW-SODIUM

This chutney can be eaten for breakfast, like marmalade, slathered on toast. And while it seems this recipe calls for a lot of sugar, you will not find the chutney overly sweet. For extra heat, use smoked chipotle chile powder and add a dash or two of cayenne. Select bright colored, unblemished limes with thin smooth skins. The freshest and juiciest limes will give slightly when you squeeze them.

PREP TIME: 10 minutes
COOK TIME: 1 hour 10 minutes
PROCESSING TIME: 20 minutes
TOTAL TIME: 1 hour, 40 minutes

12 limes, scrubbed and cut into ½-inch dice
12 garlic cloves, thinly sliced lengthwise
1 (4-inch) piece fresh ginger, peeled and thinly sliced
8 green chile peppers (jalapeños or serranos), stemmed, seeded, and thinly sliced
1 tablespoon chili powder
1 cup distilled white vinegar
¾ cup sugar

1. Prepare a hot water bath (see page 30). Place the jars in it to keep warm. Wash the lids and rings in hot, soapy water, and set aside.

2. In a medium saucepan, combine the limes, garlic, ginger, chiles, and chili powder, stir well, and bring to a simmer.

3. Add the vinegar and sugar, return to a simmer, and cook, stirring occasionally, until the limes are tender and the mixture is thick enough to mound when dropped from a spoon, about 70 minutes. Remove from the heat.

4. Ladle the chutney into the prepared jars, leaving ¼ inch of headspace. Use a nonmetallic utensil to release any air bubbles. Wipe the rims clean and seal with the lids and rings.

5. Process the jars in a hot water bath (see page 31) for 20 minutes. Turn off the heat and let the jars rest in the water bath for 10 minutes.

6. Carefully remove the jars from the hot water canner. Set aside to cool for 12 hours.

7. Check the lids for proper seals (see page 32). Remove the rings, wipe the jars, label and date them, and transfer to a cupboard or pantry.

8. For the best flavor, allow the chutney to rest for 3 days before serving. Refrigerate any jars that don't seal properly, and use within 6 weeks. Properly sealed jars will last in the cupboard for 12 months. Once opened, refrigerate and consume within 6 weeks.

SPICY TOMATO CHUTNEY

MAKES 4 HALF-PINT JARS

WATER-BATH CANNING

This tomato chutney is not the typical sweet variety, but instead a spicy, aromatic one well suited to a firm piece of bread and a fragrant, firm cheese. Serve it with meats for a spicy and surprising accompaniment, or slather it on a sandwich for added personality. Start with the recommended amount of sugar and increase the amount if the balance is not correct for your particular tomatoes.

PREP TIME: 20 minutes
COOK TIME: 1 hour, 40 minutes
PROCESSING TIME: 15 minutes
TOTAL TIME: 2 hours, 15 minutes

- 1 teaspoon cumin seeds
- 1 teaspoon black mustard seeds
- 1 teaspoon coriander seeds
- 1 teaspoon fennel seeds
- 4 dried chiles
- ½ teaspoon red pepper flakes
- 2 cups white vinegar
- ½ cup sugar
- 8 cups peeled, chopped, and drained Roma or other paste tomatoes
- 12 garlic cloves, chopped
- 1 teaspoon pickling salt

1. In a hot, dry skillet, combine the cumin seeds, mustard seeds, coriander seeds, fennel seeds, and chiles. Toast the spices, stirring continuously, until fragrant. Transfer the spices to a small bowl. Add the red pepper flakes. Set aside.

2. In a large pot set over medium heat, combine the white vinegar and sugar. Bring to a simmer, stirring to dissolve the sugar.

3. Add the tomatoes, reserved spices, and garlic. Bring to a boil. Reduce the heat to medium. Simmer for about 1½ hours, or until thickened. Stir occasionally at first and more frequently as it thickens. Once thickened, stir in the pickling salt and remove from the heat.

4. Prepare a hot water bath (see page 30). Place the jars in it to keep warm. Wash the lids and rings in hot, soapy water, and set aside.

5. Ladle the chutney into the prepared jars, leaving ½ inch of headspace. Use a nonmetallic utensil to release any air bubbles. Wipe the rims clean and seal with the lids and rings.

6. Process the jars in a hot water bath (see page 31) for 15 minutes. Turn off the heat and let the jars rest in the water bath for 10 minutes.

7. Carefully remove the jars from the hot water canner. Set aside to cool for 12 hours.

8. Check the lids for proper seals (see page 32). Remove the rings, wipe the jars, label and date them, and transfer to a cupboard or pantry.

9. For the best flavor, allow the chutney to cure for 3 to 4 weeks before serving. Refrigerate any jars that don't seal properly, and use within 6 weeks. Properly sealed jars will last in the cupboard for 12 months. Once opened, refrigerate and consume within 6 weeks.

CLOSER LOOK

Depending on the type of dried chile you use, the heat profile of this recipe will vary. For a very spicy taste, choose Thai or habañero chiles. Ancho, cascabel, or California chiles are good choices to produce a milder heat.

7

CANNED FRUITS & VEGETABLES

The wonderful thing about canning fruits and vegetables is that you are able to put the control in your hands, creating a finished product that minimizes sugar and salt, while retaining the same great flavor. Packed with water-bath and pressure canning projects, this chapter provides an assortment of recipes for staples that you can enjoy all year long.

PEACHES IN LIGHT SYRUP

MAKES 5 PINT JARS

WATER-BATH CANNING

One of the joys of preserving your own food is that you can prepare foods exactly how you like them. This summer peach recipe provides a low-sugar alternative to the canned peaches found at the store, making the end result "just peachy." Highlighting the flavor of ripe peaches, this simple recipe tastes of summer nostalgia all year long. Select freestone peaches, which are much easier to prepare than clingstone varieties.

PREP TIME: 20 minutes
COOK TIME: 5 minutes
PROCESSING TIME: 25 minutes
TOTAL TIME: 50 minutes

2 tablespoons freshly squeezed lemon juice
4¾ cups water, divided
4 pounds peaches, peeled and halved
1¼ cups sugar

1. Prepare a hot water bath (see page 30). Place the jars in it to keep warm. Wash the lids and rings in hot, soapy water, and set aside.

2. In a large bowl, combine the lemon juice with 2½ cups of water. As you prepare the peaches, immediately place them in the lemon water to prevent browning. Continue to mix the peaches in the lemon water as you go.

3. Drain the halved peaches from the lemon water. Pack into the prepared jars, cavity-side down, leaving 1 inch of headspace.

4. In a medium saucepan set over medium-high heat, combine the remaining 2¼ cups of water and the sugar. Bring to a boil.

5. Ladle the syrup into the packed jars, leaving ½ inch of headspace. Use a nonmetallic utensil to release any air bubbles. Wipe the rims clean and seal with the lids and rings.

6. Process the jars in a hot water bath (see page 31) for 25 minutes. Turn off the heat and let the jars rest in the water bath for 10 minutes.

7. Carefully remove the jars from the hot water canner. Set aside to cool for 12 hours.

8. Check the lids for proper seals (see page 32). Remove the rings, wipe the jars, label and date them, and transfer to a cupboard or pantry.

9. Refrigerate any jars that don't seal properly, and use within 3 weeks. Properly sealed jars will last in the cupboard for 12 months. Once opened, refrigerate and consume within 3 weeks.

LOW-SUGAR PREPARATION TIP

While this recipe is already a low-sugar recipe, you can adapt it further to suit your needs. Reduce the sugar as desired, or omit it altogether. If you are canning peaches in just water, bring the water to a boil before filling the jars.

CLOSER LOOK

There are many types of peaches to choose from at the height of the summer. Depending on where you live, your selection will vary. Some of the best, sweetest, and juiciest varieties for canning are Elberta, Fairhaven, Redhaven, Red Globe, and Sun High.

VANILLA NECTARINES IN SYRUP

MAKES 5 PINT JARS

WATER-BATH CANNING

Nectarines are one of the simplest fruits to can whole because, unlike many other fruits, they do not need to be peeled for canning. Select ripe fruits with few blemishes for the best flavor and presentation in the jar.

PREP TIME: 20 minutes
COOK TIME: 5 minutes
PROCESSING TIME: 25 minutes
TOTAL TIME: 50 minutes

2 tablespoons freshly squeezed lemon juice
4¾ cups water, divided
4 pounds nectarines, halved and pitted
1 whole vanilla bean, split lengthwise and cut into smaller pieces
1¾ cups sugar

1. Prepare a hot water bath (see page 30). Place the jars in it to keep warm. Wash the lids and rings in hot, soapy water, and set aside.

2. In a large bowl, combine the lemon juice with 2½ cups of water. As you prepare the nectarines, immediately place them in the lemon water to prevent browning. Continue to mix the nectarines in the lemon water as you go.

3. Drain the prepared nectarines from the lemon water. Pack into the prepared jars, cavity-side down, leaving 1 inch of headspace.

4. Evenly divide the vanilla bean pieces among the jars.

5. In a medium saucepan set over medium-high heat, combine the remaining 2¼ cups of water and sugar. Bring to a boil.

6. Ladle the syrup into the packed jars, leaving ½ inch of headspace. Use a nonmetallic utensil to release any air bubbles. Wipe the rims clean and seal with the lids and rings. Process the jars in a hot water bath (see page 31) for 25 minutes. Turn off the heat and let the jars rest in the water bath for 10 minutes.

7. Carefully remove the jars from the hot water canner. Set aside to cool for 12 hours.

8. Check the lids for proper seals (see page 32). Remove the rings, wipe the jars, label and date them, and transfer to a cupboard or pantry.

9. Refrigerate any jars that don't seal properly, and use within 3 weeks. Properly sealed jars will last in the cupboard for 12 months. Once opened, refrigerate and consume within 3 weeks.

LOW-SUGAR PREPARATION TIP

This recipe has a slightly higher sugar content than Peaches in Light Syrup (see page 152). If you prefer a lighter syrup, substitute the one in that recipe for the one here. You can make it even lighter by using as little as ¾ cup of sugar for an extra-light syrup. Peaches and nectarines can be canned with water, but using a sugar syrup, even a light or extra-light one, adds plumpness to the fruit as well as flavor.

SPICED PLUMS IN SYRUP

MAKES 4 PINT JARS

WATER-BATH CANNING, SEASONAL

Plums are another time-saving winner in canning as they can be canned whole. Use small wild plums or cultivated varieties that are on the smaller side and typically available in late summer. If you can't find any small plums, use a larger variety but halve and pit them for this recipe. When you've filled the jars, don't toss the syrup—use it to flavor your favorite cocktail, "mocktail," or even a glass of sparkling water.

PREP TIME: 5 minutes
COOK TIME: 15 minutes, plus overnight resting time
PROCESSING TIME: 25 minutes
TOTAL TIME: 45 minutes, plus overnight resting time

4 pounds small plums, washed
3 cups sugar
½ cup white vinegar
4 cinnamon sticks
4 whole cloves
4 allspice berries

DAY 1

1. With a skewer, poke each plum two times on opposite sides to prevent splitting. Pack into a small crock or other food-safe container.

2. In a medium saucepot, combine the sugar, white vinegar, cinnamon sticks, cloves, and allspice. Bring to a boil. Reduce the heat to low. Simmer for 5 minutes. Pour the syrup over the plums.

3. Cover with a clean kitchen towel. Let stand overnight at room temperature.

DAY 2

1. Prepare a hot water bath (see page 30). Place the jars in it to keep warm. Wash the lids and rings in hot, soapy water, and set aside.

2. Drain the plums, reserving the syrup. Pack into the prepared jars, leaving 1 inch of headspace.

3. In a medium saucepan set over medium-high heat, bring the reserved syrup to a boil. Ladle the hot syrup into the packed jars, leaving ½ inch of headspace.

4. From the reserved syrup, remove and place 1 cinnamon stick, 1 clove, and 1 allspice berry into each jar. Use a nonmetallic utensil to release any air bubbles. Wipe the rims clean and seal with the lids and rings.

Continued

SPICED PLUMS IN SYRUP

CONTINUED

5. Process the jars in a hot water bath (see page 31) for 25 minutes. Turn off the heat and let the jars rest in the water bath for 10 minutes.

6. Carefully remove the jars from the hot water canner. Set aside to cool for 12 hours.

7. Check the lids for proper seals (see page 32). Remove the rings, wipe the jars, label and date them, and transfer to a cupboard or pantry.

8. Refrigerate any jars that don't seal properly, and use within 3 weeks. Properly sealed jars will last in the cupboard for 12 months. Once opened, refrigerate and consume within 3 weeks.

SPICED PEARS IN SYRUP

MAKES 4 PINT JARS

WATER-BATH CANNING

Commercially canned pears are packed in a thick syrup that can be cloyingly sweet. This version, made with a light syrup, is far from ordinary. With an aromatic, flavorful combination of cinnamon, cloves, and vanilla, the star of the show—the pear—can be enjoyed for all its worth.

PREP TIME: 20 minutes
COOK TIME: 5 minutes
PROCESSING TIME: 20 minutes
TOTAL TIME: 45 minutes

- 2 tablespoons freshly squeezed lemon juice
- 5 cups water, divided
- 5 pounds pears, peeled, cored, and halved, quartered, or sliced, as desired
- 1¾ cups sugar
- 1 teaspoon pure vanilla extract
- 4 cinnamon sticks, divided
- 4 whole cloves, divided

1. Prepare a hot water bath (see page 30). Place the jars in it to keep warm. Wash the lids and rings in hot, soapy water, and set aside.

2. In a large bowl, combine the lemon juice with 2½ cups of water. As you prepare the pears, immediately place them in the lemon water to prevent browning. Continue to mix the pears in the lemon water as you go.

3. Drain the prepared pears from the lemon water well. Set aside.

4. In a large saucepot set over medium-high heat, combine the remaining 2½ cups of water, sugar, and vanilla. Bring to a boil. Reduce the heat to keep warm. Add the pears.

5. To each jar, add 1 cinnamon stick and 1 clove.

6. Ladle the pears and syrup into the prepared jars, leaving ½ inch of headspace. Use a nonmetallic utensil to release any air bubbles. Wipe the rims clean and seal with the lids and rings.

7. Process the jars in a hot water bath (see page 31) for 20 minutes. Turn off the heat and let the jars rest in the water bath for 10 minutes.

8. Carefully remove the jars from the hot water canner. Set aside to cool for 12 hours.

Continued

SPICED PEARS IN SYRUP

CONTINUED

9. Check the lids for proper seals (see page 32). Remove the rings, wipe the jars, label and date them, and transfer to a cupboard or pantry.

10. Refrigerate any jars that don't seal properly, and use within 3 weeks. Properly sealed jars will last in the cupboard for 12 months. Once opened, refrigerate and consume within 3 weeks.

LOW-SUGAR PREPARATION TIP

This recipe can be adapted using less sugar to save on calories. If you plan to add no sugar, substitute water in place of the syrup. Because of the added flavor that even an extra-light syrup imparts, it's recommended that you add at least ½ cup of sugar to the water to create a very light syrup and slightly plumper fruit. Alternatively, fruit juice can be used in place of syrup.

CLOSER LOOK

Bartlett pears are widely considered one of the best varieties for canning, but Comice, Bosc, Anjou, and Seckel pears all produce great results. If you don't mind the skin, leave it on. Be cautious using Asian pears, though, which are low in acid. When using this type of pear for canning, it is imperative to acidify the fruit by adding 1 tablespoon of bottled lemon juice to each pint.

ROASTED PEPPERS

MAKES 4 PINT JARS

PRESSURE CANNING

Peppers and chiles of all sorts can be canned in a pressure canner. If you don't want to bother with roasting, peeling, and seeding, you can just cut a few slits in the peppers and leave them whole. The peppers are safe to eat as long as they are processed properly in a pressure canner. You can simply pull away the skin and seeds once you open the jar to use them.

PREP TIME: 15 minutes
COOK TIME: 20 minutes
PROCESSING TIME: 35 minutes
TOTAL TIME: 1 hour, 10 minutes

4 pounds peppers, any variety or a combination
2 teaspoons kosher salt, divided (optional)

1. Preheat the oven to 400°F.

2. Pierce the peppers with a fork or paring knife in two or three places. Place them on a baking sheet. Roast in the preheated oven for 15 to 20 minutes, turning occasionally, until very tender and the skins look wrinkled.

3. Cool the peppers until you can handle them. Pull away the skins. Remove the stems and seeds.

4. Wash the jars, lids, and rings in hot, soapy water, and set aside.

5. Place a rack in a pressure canner and add 3 to 4 inches of water. Fill the jars with a couple inches of water so they do not float. Place them in the canner. Bring the water in the canner to a simmer until ready to fill the jars. *Do not boil the water.*

6. Bring a pot of fresh water to a boil.

7. Remove the jars from the canner, empty into the sink, and place them on a cutting board on a nearby countertop.

8. Pack the roasted peppers into the jars, leaving 1 inch of headspace. Add ½ teaspoon of kosher salt to each jar (if using).

9. Cover the peppers with boiling water, leaving 1 inch of headspace. Use a nonmetallic utensil to release any air bubbles. Wipe the rims clean and seal with the lids and rings.

Continued

ROASTED PEPPERS

CONTINUED

10. Put the jars on the rack in the pressure canner. Lock the lid in place, bring to a boil, and let the canner vent for 10 minutes. Put the weighted gauge or pressure regulator on the vent.

11. Process for 35 minutes at 11 pounds on a dial gauge or at 10 pounds on a weighted gauge. Adjust the pressure as necessary based on your altitude (see page 233). Adjust the temperature to maintain an even pressure. Turn off the heat. Let the pressure drop to zero before opening the lid.

12. Carefully remove the jars from the canner. Set aside to cool, undisturbed, for 12 hours.

13. Check the lids for proper seals (see page 32). Remove the rings, wipe the jars, label and date them, and transfer to a cupboard or pantry.

14. Refrigerate any jars that don't seal properly, and use within 5 days. Properly sealed jars will last in the cupboard for 12 months. Once opened, refrigerate and consume within 5 days.

STEWED TOMATOES AND OKRA

MAKES 8 PINT JARS, OR 4 QUART JARS

PRESSURE CANNING

Capture the bright colors and textures of late summer with this classic recipe. Fresh okra is low in acid, which means hot water-bath canning is not appropriate. This is a great reason to bring out your pressure canner. These savory vegetables can be the perfect side dish or the star of the plate, served over rice or stirred into a gumbo or jambalaya.

PREP TIME: 30 minutes
COOK TIME: 30 minutes
PROCESSING TIME: 30 minutes for pints; 35 minutes for quarts
TOTAL TIME: 1 hour, 35 minutes

7 pounds tomatoes
2½ pounds okra, trimmed and cut into 1-inch-thick slices
4 teaspoons kosher salt, divided (optional)

1. Place a large pot of water over high heat and bring to a rolling boil.

2. Cut a small X through the blossom end of the tomatoes. Blanch them in the boiling water for 1 to 2 minutes, in batches, or until the skins begin to curl, depending on ripeness of the tomatoes. With a slotted spoon, transfer them to an ice bath to stop the cooking. Drain. Repeat with the remaining tomatoes.

3. Remove the skins and cut the tomatoes into chunks.

4. Wash the jars, lids, and rings in hot, soapy water, and set aside.

5. Place a rack in a pressure canner and add 3 to 4 inches of water. Fill the jars with a couple inches of water so they do not float. Place them in the canner. Bring the water to a simmer until ready to fill the jars. *Do not boil the water.*

6. In a preserving pot or a saucepot set over medium heat, bring the tomatoes to a simmer. Cook for 10 minutes.

7. Add the okra. Continue to cook for about 5 minutes more, or until the okra is just barely tender.

8. Remove the jars from the canner, empty into the sink, and place them on a cutting board on a nearby countertop.

Continued

STEWED TOMATOES AND OKRA
CONTINUED

9. Add ½ teaspoon of kosher salt to each pint jar, or 1 teaspoon of salt to each quart jar (if using).

10. Ladle the tomatoes and okra into the prepared jars, leaving 1 inch of headspace. Use a nonmetallic utensil to release any air bubbles. Wipe the rims clean and seal with the lids and rings.

11. Put the jars on the rack in the pressure canner. Lock the lid in place, bring to a boil, and let the canner vent for 10 minutes. Put the weighted gauge or pressure regulator on the vent.

12. Process pints for 30 minutes, or quarts for 35 minutes at 11 pounds on a dial gauge or at 10 pounds on a weighted gauge. Adjust the pressure as necessary based on your altitude (see page 233). Adjust the temperature to maintain an even pressure. Turn off the heat. Let the pressure drop to zero before opening the lid.

13. Carefully remove the jars from the canner. Set aside to cool, undisturbed, for 12 hours.

14. Check the lids for proper seals (see page 32). Remove the rings, wipe the jars, label and date them, and transfer to a cupboard or pantry.

15. Refrigerate any jars that don't seal properly, and use within 3 days. Properly sealed jars will last in the cupboard for 12 months. Once opened, refrigerate and consume within 3 days.

TRY INSTEAD

There are several flavoring options you can use to season this recipe and create your own house brand. Try a taste of the Mediterranean with spices like cardamom or rosemary, or add the warmth of India with coriander and turmeric.

WHOLE TOMATOES

MAKES 6 PINT JARS

WATER-BATH CANNING, LOW-SODIUM

If there is just one pantry staple to can this summer, whole tomatoes is it. Simple to make and infinitely versatile, whole tomatoes work well in soups, stews, and casseroles. Cook them down into a chunky sauce, or purée them for a creamy soup base. Whatever you do with them, make plenty when the season is in high swing, so you have a stocked pantry all winter long.

PREP TIME: 30 minutes
COOK TIME: 10 minutes
PROCESSING TIME: 40 minutes
TOTAL TIME: 1 hour, 20 minutes

10 pounds Roma or other paste tomatoes
6 tablespoons bottled lemon juice, divided

1. Prepare a hot water bath (see page 30). Place the jars in it to keep warm. Wash the lids and rings in hot, soapy water, and set aside.

2. Place a large pot of water over high heat and bring to a rolling boil.

3. Core the tomatoes and cut a small X through the blossom end. Working in batches, blanch the tomatoes in the boiling water for 1 to 2 minutes, or until the skins begin to curl, depending on ripeness of the tomatoes. With a slotted spoon, immediately transfer to an ice bath to stop the cooking. Drain. Repeat with the remaining tomatoes.

4. Slip the skins off the cooled tomatoes. Discard the skins, or save to make Vegetable Stock (see page 180).

5. Bring a pot of fresh water to a boil.

6. Add 1 tablespoon of lemon juice to each jar.

7. Pack the tomatoes into the prepared jars, lightly pressing them to fill, but without mashing.

8. Ladle boiling water over, completely covering the tomatoes, leaving ½ inch of headspace. Use a nonmetallic utensil to remove any air bubbles, adjusting the headspace with more water, as needed. Wipe the rims clean and seal with the lids and rings.

Continued

WHOLE TOMATOES

CONTINUED

9. Process the jars in a hot water bath (see page 31) for 40 minutes. Turn off the heat and let the jars rest in the water bath for 10 minutes.

10. Carefully remove the jars from the hot water canner. Set aside to cool for 12 hours.

11. Check the lids for proper seals (see page 32). Remove the rings, wipe the jars, label and date them, and transfer to a cupboard or pantry.

12. Refrigerate any jars that don't seal properly, and use within 5 days. Properly sealed jars will last in the cupboard for 12 months. Once opened, refrigerate and consume within 5 days.

TRY INSTEAD

You can hot-pack these tomatoes. Place the peeled tomatoes in a pot and add enough water to cover. Simmer for 5 minutes. Transfer the tomatoes and their cooking liquid to the jars, leaving ½ inch of headspace. Process in a water-bath canner for 40 minutes.

CANNED CREAMED CORN

MAKES 6 PINT JARS

PRESSURE CANNING, LOW-SODIUM

Despite its name, the only cream in this corn comes from scraping the cobs to extract their milky, flavorful liquid. Creamed corn is a delicious side dish whether served on its own or turned into a baked gratin with a crunchy breaded topping. Corn and peppers, or chiles, make a great flavor combination. Add sweet bell peppers or hot chiles to taste.

PREP TIME: 10 minutes
COOK TIME: 30 minutes
PROCESSING TIME: 1 hour, 30 minutes
TOTAL TIME: 2 hours, 10 minutes

2½ dozen (½ bushel) ears of corn, husked
Water
Salt, for seasoning (optional)

1. Bring a large pot (or two) of water to a rolling boil. Add the corn. Cook for 3 to 4 minutes, in batches, until tender. Drain and let cool. Repeat until all corn is cooked and cooled.

2. Working inside a large bowl where you can easily handle the corn, use a paring knife to cut away the kernels. Then, scrape the knife down the cob to release the juices.

3. Prepare the jars, lids, and rings by washing them in hot, soapy water and set aside.

4. Place a rack in a pressure canner and add 3 to 4 inches of water. Fill the jars with a couple inches of water so they do not float, and place them in the canner. Bring the water to a simmer until ready to fill the jars. Do not boil the water.

5. Bring a large pot of fresh water to a boil.

6. Measure the corn and its milk into another large bowl—for every 2 cups of corn, add 1 cup of boiling water.

7. Remove the jars from the canner, empty into the sink, and place them on a cutting board on a nearby countertop.

8. Ladle the corn mixture into the prepared jars, leaving ½ inch of headspace. Use a nonmetallic utensil to release any air bubbles. Wipe the rims clean and seal with the lids and rings.

Continued

CANNED CREAMED CORN

CONTINUED

9. Put the jars on a rack in the pressure canner. Lock the lid in place, bring to a boil, and let the canner vent for 10 minutes. Put the weighted gauge or pressure regulator on the vent.

10. Process for 1 hour, 30 minutes at 11 pounds on a dial gauge or at 10 pounds on a weighted gauge. Adjust the pressure as necessary based on your altitude (see page 233). Adjust the temperature to maintain an even pressure. Turn off the heat. Let the pressure drop to zero before opening the lid.

11. Carefully remove the jars from the canner. Set aside to cool, undisturbed, for 12 hours.

12. Check the lids for proper seals (see page 32). Remove the rings, wipe the jars, label and date them, and transfer to a cupboard or pantry.

13. Refrigerate any jars that don't seal properly, and use within 3 days. Properly sealed jars will last in the cupboard for 12 months. Once opened, refrigerate and consume within 3 days.

TOMATO JUICE COCKTAIL (OR BLOODY MARY MIX)

MAKES 5 QUART JARS

PRESSURE CANNING

If you enjoy vegetable juices like tomato juice or vegetable blends, making your own is simple and lets you control the flavor. Leave it plain and simple for a refreshing low-calorie, high-fiber drink, or spike it with pepper and horseradish for the ultimate Bloody Mary. You can also lower the sodium compared to store-bought versions, which are often packed with salt and other preservatives.

PREP TIME: 30 minutes
COOK TIME: 30 minutes
PROCESSING TIME: 35 minutes
TOTAL TIME: 1 hour, 35 minutes

15 pounds tomatoes, cored and chopped
4 celery stalks, chopped
1 yellow onion, chopped
2 beets, peeled and chopped
3 tablespoons Worcestershire sauce
2 tablespoons sugar
1 tablespoon prepared horseradish (optional)
1 tablespoon canning salt
½ teaspoon freshly ground black pepper
½ teaspoon hot sauce
½ teaspoon seasoning salt
10 tablespoons bottled lemon juice, divided

1. Prepare the jars, lids, and rings by washing them in hot, soapy water.

2. Place a rack in a pressure canner and add 3 to 4 inches of water. Fill the jars with a couple inches of water so they do not float, and place them in the canner. Bring the water to a simmer until ready to fill the jars. *Do not boil the water.*

3. In a large saucepot (or two) set over medium heat, crush the tomatoes with a potato masher or wooden spoon, in batches, until all are incorporated. Bring to a simmer. Cook for about 5 minutes, stirring frequently, or until very tender.

4. Add the celery, onion, and beets. Simmer for 15 to 20 minutes, or until tender.

5. In a food processor or blender, purée the mixture until smooth.

6. Into a clean saucepot, strain the mixture through a fine mesh sieve. Use a spatula to press out as much juice as possible. Discard the skins, seeds, and fiber.

7. Return the pot to the stove over medium heat and bring to a simmer. Add the Worcestershire sauce, sugar, horseradish (if using), canning salt, pepper, hot sauce, and seasoning salt. Continue to simmer for 5 minutes.

Continued

TOMATO JUICE COCKTAIL (OR BLOODY MARY MIX)

CONTINUED

8. Remove the jars from the canner, empty into the sink, and place them on a cutting board on a nearby countertop.

9. Measure 2 tablespoons of lemon juice into each jar.

10. Ladle the vegetable juice into the prepared jars, leaving 1 inch of headspace. Use a nonmetallic utensil to release any air bubbles. Wipe the rims clean and seal with the lids and rings.

11. Put the jars on a rack in the pressure canner. Lock the lid in place, bring to a boil, and let the canner vent for 10 minutes. Put the weighted gauge or pressure regulator on the vent.

12. Process for 35 minutes at 11 pounds on a dial gauge or at 10 pounds on a weighted gauge. Adjust the pressure as necessary based on your altitude (see page 233). Adjust the temperature as necessary to maintain an even pressure. Turn off the heat and let the pressure drop to zero before removing the lid.

13. Carefully remove the jars from the canner. Set aside to cool, undisturbed, for 12 hours.

14. Check the lids for proper seals (see page 32). Remove the rings, wipe the jars, label and date them, and transfer to a cupboard or pantry.

15. Refrigerate any jars that don't seal properly, and use within 2 months. Properly sealed jars will last in the cupboard for 12 months. Once opened, refrigerate and consume within 2 months.

LOW-SODIUM PREPARATION TIP

This juice has a lot less sodium than any commercially available tomato juice. However, if you wish to cut the sodium further, omit both the seasoning salt and canning salt. Or add just a small amount, about ½ teaspoon per jar, at the time of canning.

DRIED BEANS

MAKES 5 PINT JARS

PRESSURE CANNING, LOW-SODIUM

While canned beans are readily available, making them at home has its benefits. First is the cost savings. Seems impossible considering how inexpensive canned beans are, but buying them dried is even cheaper. You also cut a great deal of waste with reusable canning jars. More compelling, though, is you can leave out the salt—the end result is not teeming with sodium like typical canned varieties. Use any type of dried beans, including black, kidney, pinto, Great Northern, or navy beans, and be ready with plenty of options for a quick, nutritious meal.

PREP TIME: 5 minutes
COOK TIME: 35 minutes, plus 1 hour soaking time
PROCESSING TIME: 1 hour, 15 minutes
TOTAL TIME: 2 hours, 55 minutes

2 pounds dried beans
Water
2½ teaspoons salt, divided (optional)

1. In a large pot set over medium-high, combine the beans with enough water to cover by 2 inches. Bring to a boil. Cook for 2 minutes. Remove the pot from the heat, cover, and let sit for 1 hour.

2. Prepare the jars, lids, and rings by washing them in hot, soapy water.

3. Place a rack in a pressure canner and add 3 to 4 inches of water. Fill the jars with a couple inches of water so they do not float, and place them in the canner. Bring the water to a simmer until ready to fill the jars. *Do not boil the water.*

4. Drain the beans, return them to the pot, and, again, cover with 2 inches of water. Bring to a boil over high heat. Cook for 30 minutes, stirring frequently.

5. Remove the jars from the canner, empty into the sink, and place them on a cutting board on a nearby countertop.

6. Ladle the hot beans into the prepared jars, leaving 1 inch of headspace. Add ½ teaspoon of salt to each jar (if using). Cover the beans with the hot cooking liquid, leaving 1 inch of headspace. Use a nonmetallic utensil to release any air bubbles. Wipe the rims clean and seal with the lids and rings.

7. Put the jars on a rack in the pressure canner. Lock the lid in place, bring to a boil, and let the canner vent for 10 minutes. Put the weighted gauge or pressure regulator on the vent.

Continued

DRIED BEANS

CONTINUED

8. Process for 1 hour, 15 minutes at 11 pounds on a dial gauge or at 10 pounds on a weighted gauge. Adjust the pressure as necessary based on your altitude (see page 233). Adjust the temperature as necessary to maintain an even pressure. Turn off the heat. Let the pressure drop to zero before opening the lid.

9. Carefully remove the jars from the canner. Set aside to cool, undisturbed, for 12 hours.

10. Check the lids for proper seals (see page 32). Remove the rings, wipe the jars, label and date them, and transfer to a cupboard or pantry.

11. Refrigerate any jars that don't seal properly, and use within 5 days. Properly sealed jars will last in the cupboard for 12 months. Once opened, refrigerate and consume within 5 days.

SWEET POTATOES

MAKES 6 PINT JARS

PRESSURE CANNING

Opening a can of cooked sweet potatoes is super quick on a day where you don't have time to cook. Follow this simple preparation to create lightly sweetened sweet potato chunks that can be used to make soups or baked into casseroles at a moment's notice.

PREP TIME: 10 minutes
COOK TIME: 20 minutes
PROCESSING TIME: 1 hour, 5 minutes
TOTAL TIME: 1 hour, 35 minutes

8 pounds sweet potatoes, scrubbed well
1¼ cups sugar
5½ cups water, plus additional for boiling

1. Prepare the jars, lids, and rings by washing them in hot, soapy water.

2. Place a rack in a pressure canner and add 3 to 4 inches of water. Fill the jars with a couple inches of water so they do not float, and place them in the canner. Bring the water to a simmer until ready to fill the jars. *Do not boil the water.*

3. Bring a large pot of water to a rolling boil. Add the sweet potatoes. Cook for about 15 minutes, or until the skins can be easily removed. Remove from the heat and drain. When cool enough to handle, slip them from their skins. Cube the sweet potatoes.

4. Remove the jars from the canner, empty into the sink, and place them on a cutting board on a nearby countertop.

5. While still hot, pack the sweet potatoes into the prepared jars, leaving 1 inch of headspace.

6. In a medium saucepan set over medium-high heat, combine the sugar and 5½ cups of water. Bring to a boil.

7. Ladle the hot syrup into the jars, leaving 1 inch of headspace. Use a nonmetallic utensil to release any air bubbles. Wipe the rims clean and seal with the lids and rings.

8. Put the jars on a rack in the pressure canner. Lock the lid in place, bring the water to a boil, and let the canner vent for 10 minutes. Put the weighted gauge or pressure regulator on the vent.

Continued

SWEET POTATOES

CONTINUED

9. Process for 1 hour, 5 minutes at 11 pounds on a dial gauge or at 10 pounds on a weighted gauge. Adjust the pressure as needed based on your altitude (see page 233). Adjust the temperature as necessary to maintain an even pressure. Turn off the heat. Let the pressure drop to zero before opening the lid.

10. Carefully remove the jars from the canner. Set aside to cool, undisturbed, for 12 hours.

11. Check the lids for proper seals (see page 32). Remove the rings, wipe the jars, label and date them, and transfer to a cupboard or pantry.

12. Refrigerate any jars that don't seal properly, and use within 2 months. Properly sealed jars will last in the cupboard for 12 months. Once opened, refrigerate and consume within 2 months.

LOW-SUGAR PREPARATION TIP

Make this a no-added-sugar recipe by omitting the syrup and, instead, use boiling water as the canning liquid. The difference in the finished product will be negligible, but this simple omission gives you the great taste of sweet potatoes without the added calories.

CLOSER LOOK

Vegetables like sweet potatoes cannot be safely processed when mashed. The texture is too thick and does not allow the heat to penetrate adequately. Since these are fully cooked when canned, once opened, they can easily be mashed or puréed as needed for your dish.

SWEET PEAS

MAKES 6 PINT JARS

PRESSURE CANNING, LOW-SODIUM

The most time-consuming task when canning peas is shelling them. Pull up a comfy chair, a cool beverage, and some good company to make the process go quickly. While English peas and other varieties of shelling peas are great canned, don't be tempted to can whole pea pods, such as snow or sugar snap peas, as these produce poor results.

PREP TIME: 1 hour
COOK TIME: 5 minutes
PROCESSING TIME: 40 minutes
TOTAL TIME: 1 hour, 45 minutes

14 pounds shelling peas, shelled and rinsed
Water
3 teaspoons salt, divided (optional)

1. Prepare the jars, lids, and rings by washing them in hot, soapy water.

2. Place a rack in a pressure canner and add 3 to 4 inches of water. Fill the jars with a couple inches of water so they do not float, and place them in the canner. Bring the water to a simmer until ready to fill the jars. *Do not boil the water.*

3. In a large pot, combine the peas with enough water to cover. Bring to a boil. Cook for 2 minutes. Turn off the heat. Drain, reserving the cooking water.

4. Remove the jars from the canner, empty into the sink, and place them on a cutting board on a nearby countertop.

5. Pack the peas into the prepared jars, leaving 1 inch of headspace. Add ½ teaspoon of salt to each jar (if using). Cover the peas with the reserved cooking water, leaving 1 inch of headspace. Use a nonmetallic utensil to release any air bubbles. Wipe the rims clean and seal with the lids and rings.

6. Put the jars on a rack in the pressure canner. Lock the lid in place, bring the water to a boil, and let the canner vent for 10 minutes. Put the weighted gauge or pressure regulator on the vent.

Continued

SWEET PEAS
CONTINUED

7. Process for 40 minutes at 11 pounds on a dial gauge or at 10 pounds on a weighted gauge. Adjust the pressure as necessary based on your altitude (see page 233). Adjust the temperature to maintain an even pressure. Turn off the heat. Let the pressure drop to zero before opening the lid.

8. Carefully remove the jars from the canner. Set aside to cool, undisturbed, for 12 hours.

9. Check the lids for proper seals (see page 32). Remove the rings, wipe the jars, label and date them, and transfer to a cupboard or pantry.

10. Refrigerate any jars that don't seal properly, and use within 3 days. Properly sealed jars will last in the cupboard for 12 months. Once opened, refrigerate and consume within 3 days.

BEETS

MAKES 6 PINT JARS

PRESSURE CANNING, LOW-SODIUM

Canned beets are an earthy, tasty, colorful addition to the pantry. Use them for salads and dips to bring some bright color to the meal. Wear gloves when working with them, especially if you have any plans later in the day, as they will surely leave your hands a bright red color.

PREP TIME: 20 minutes
COOK TIME: 25 minutes
PROCESSING TIME: 30 minutes
TOTAL TIME: 1 hour, 15 minutes

12 pounds beets, greens removed, leaving about 1 inch of the stems and the whole roots intact
Water
3 teaspoons salt, divided (optional)

1. Prepare the jars, lids, and rings by washing them in hot, soapy water.

2. Place a rack in a pressure canner and add 3 to 4 inches of water. Fill the jars with a couple inches of water so they do not float, and place them in the canner. Bring the water to a simmer until ready to fill the jars. *Do not boil the water.*

3. In a large pot set over medium-high heat, combine the beets with enough water to cover. Bring to a boil. Cook for 20 to 25 minutes, or until the skins can be removed easily. Remove from the heat, drain, and cool.

4. Once cool enough to handle, remove the skins and trim away the roots and tops. If the beets are small, leave them whole. For larger beets, quarter, halve, or slice.

5. Bring a medium pot filled with water to a boil over high heat.

6. Remove the jars from the canner, empty into the sink, and place them on a cutting board on a nearby countertop.

7. Pack the beets into the prepared jars, leaving 1 inch of headspace. Fill the jars with the boiling water, leaving 1 inch of headspace. Add ½ teaspoon of salt to each jar (if using). Use a nonmetallic utensil to release any air bubbles. Wipe the rims clean and seal with the lids and rings.

Continued

BEETS

CONTINUED

8. Put the jars on a rack in the pressure canner. Lock the lid in place, bring the water to a boil, and let the canner vent for 10 minutes. Put the weighted gauge or pressure regulator on the vent.

9. Process for 30 minutes at 11 pounds on a dial gauge or at 10 pounds on a weighted gauge. Adjust the pressure as necessary based on your altitude (see page 233). Adjust the temperature to maintain an even pressure. Turn off the heat. Let the pressure drop to zero before opening the lid.

10. Carefully remove the jars from the canner. Set aside to cool, undisturbed, for 12 hours.

11. Check the lids for proper seals (see page 32). Remove the rings, wipe the jars, label and date them, and transfer to a cupboard or pantry.

12. Refrigerate any jars that don't seal properly, and use within 3 days. Properly sealed jars will last in the cupboard for 12 months. Once opened, refrigerate and consume within 3 days.

PAIR IT

While hummus is typically made with chickpeas, a great alternative is to use beets. Combine 1 pint of drained beets with a 1/4 cup of tahini, 1/4 cup of lemon juice, 2 garlic cloves, and 1/4 teaspoon of salt. Process the mixture in a blender or food processor for a healthy dip for bread and vegetables.

GREENS

MAKES 6 PINT JARS

PRESSURE CANNING, LOW-SODIUM

Canned greens make a healthy addition to a soup or a quick side on a busy day. Make these in the summer when your garden is overflowing or when you find a great deal at the market. You can use just one type of green or mix and match to create a colorful array on your plate.

PREP TIME: 15 minutes
COOK TIME: 5 minutes
PROCESSING TIME: 1 hour, 10 minutes
TOTAL TIME: 1 hour, 30 minutes

12 pounds greens, beet, chard, collards, kale, mustard, or a combination
Water
3 teaspoons salt, divided (optional)

1. Prepare the jars, lids, and rings by washing them in hot, soapy water.

2. Place a rack in a pressure canner and add 3 to 4 inches of water. Fill the jars with a couple inches of water so they do not float, and place them in the canner. Bring the water to a simmer until ready to fill the jars. *Do not boil the water.*

3. Wash the greens well using several changes of water. Remove and discard the thick ribs, or save for Vegetable Stock (see page 180).

4. Bring a large pot of water with a steamer basket to a boil over medium-high heat. Working in batches, steam the greens for 3 to 5 minutes, or until wilted.

5. Remove the jars from the canner, empty into the sink, and place them on a cutting board on a nearby countertop.

6. Pack the greens into the prepared jars, leaving 1 inch of headspace. Add ½ teaspoon of salt to each jar (if using). Use a nonmetallic utensil to release any air bubbles. Wipe the rims clean and seal with the lids and rings.

7. Put the jars on a rack in the pressure canner. Lock the lid in place, bring to a boil, and let the canner vent for 10 minutes. Put the weighted gauge or pressure regulator on the vent.

Continued

GREENS

CONTINUED

8. Process for 1 hour, 10 minutes at 11 pounds on a dial gauge or at 10 pounds on a weighted gauge. Adjust the pressure as necessary based on your altitude (see page 233). Adjust the temperature to maintain an even pressure. Turn off the heat. Let the pressure drop to zero before opening the lid.

9. Carefully remove the jars from the canner. Set aside to cool, undisturbed, for 12 hours.

10. Check the lids for proper seals (see page 32). Remove the rings, wipe the jars, label and date them, and transfer to a cupboard or pantry.

11. Refrigerate any jars that don't seal properly, and use within 3 days. Properly sealed jars will last in the cupboard for 12 months. Once opened, refrigerate and consume within 3 days.

LOW-SODIUM PREPARATION TIP

If you plan on eating canned greens as a side dish, salt is a nice addition though not necessary. If you will be adding them to soups, casseroles, or stews, omit the salt and instead salt the finished dish to taste.

PREPARATION TIP

The best way to clean greens is to place them all in a clean sink filled with cold water. Vigorously swirl the greens to remove as much dirt as possible. Do this once, drain the water, and repeat the process to remove most of the dirt. The second time, fill the sink and go through the greens individually, rubbing off any remaining dirt. Rinse a final time before preparing.

MOCK MINCEMEAT

MAKES 5 PINT JARS

WATER-BATH CANNING, LOW-SODIUM

True mincemeat includes meat, but this "mock" version uses green tomatoes. It's an ideal recipe to make just before the first frost threatens to take your tomato crop. The flavors develop as they rest. This will be perfectly cured, with a rich mellow flavor, by the time you need it for holiday pies and tarts.

PREP TIME: 20 minutes
COOK TIME: 1 hour
PROCESSING TIME: 10 minutes
TOTAL TIME: 1 hour, 30 minutes

2 quarts chopped green tomatoes
1 quart chopped apples
1 pound dark seedless raisins
¾ pound currants
¾ cup sugar
¾ cup firmly packed brown sugar
1 cup Pectin Stock (see page 23), or apple jelly
⅔ cup dark rum, or brandy
⅓ cup apple cider vinegar
3 tablespoons candied orange peel
2 tablespoons ground cinnamon
¼ teaspoon ground nutmeg
¼ teaspoon ground mace
¼ teaspoon ground ginger
Zest of 1 orange
Juice of 1 orange
Zest of 1 lemon
Juice of 1 lemon

1. Prepare a hot water bath (see page 30). Place the jars in it to keep warm. Wash the lids and rings in hot, soapy water, and set aside.

2. In a deep pot or preserving pot set over medium heat, stir together the tomatoes, apples, raisins, currants, sugar, brown sugar, Pectin Stock, rum, cider vinegar, candied orange peel, cinnamon, nutmeg, mace, ginger, orange zest, orange juice, lemon zest, and lemon juice. Slowly bring to a boil, stirring frequently.

3. Reduce the heat to low. Simmer for about 1 hour, or until it is very thick.

4. Ladle the mincemeat into the prepared jars, leaving ½ inch of headspace. Use a nonmetallic utensil to release any air bubbles. Wipe the rims clean and seal with the lids and rings.

5. Process the jars in a hot water bath (see page 31) for 10 minutes. Turn off the heat and let the jars rest in the water bath for 10 minutes.

6. Carefully remove the jars from the hot water canner. Set aside to cool for 12 hours.

7. Check the lids for proper seals (see page 32). Remove the rings, wipe the jars, label and date them, and transfer to a cupboard or pantry.

8. For the best flavor, allow the mincemeat to cure for 3 to 4 weeks before serving. Refrigerate any jars that don't seal properly, and use within 6 weeks. Properly sealed jars will last in the cupboard for 12 months. Once opened, refrigerate and consume within 6 weeks.

VEGETABLE STOCK

MAKES 6 PINT JARS

PRESSURE CANNING, LOW-SODIUM

Vegetable stock can be made with a variety of vegetables depending on your preference. There is no need to buy fresh vegetables for this purpose. You can easily accumulate plenty of scraps when trimming and peeling vegetables from many of this book's recipes. Store the scraps in the freezer until you have enough to make a batch. For even more flavor, use the blanching water from making creamed corn or peeling tomatoes instead of fresh water.

PREP TIME: 10 minutes
COOK TIME: 1 hour
PROCESSING TIME: 20 minutes
TOTAL TIME: 1 hour, 30 minutes

- 4 quarts water
- 1 cup carrot peels and ends
- 1 cup tomato ends
- ½ cup celery leaves and stalks
- 1 cup onion ends
- ½ cup leek ends
- 2 or 3 corn cobs
- Handful of fresh herbs: parsley, thyme, cilantro, or oregano stems

1. Prepare the jars, lids, and rings by washing them in hot, soapy water.

2. In a stockpot set over medium-high heat, combine the water, carrot, tomato, celery, onion, leek, corn cobs, and herbs. If the vegetables are frozen, there is no need to defrost them. Bring to a boil. Reduce the heat to low. Simmer for 1 hour.

3. Place a rack in a pressure canner and add 3 to 4 inches of water. Fill the jars with a couple inches of water so they do not float, and place them in the canner. Bring the water to a simmer until ready to fill the jars. *Do not boil the water.*

4. With a wire mesh strainer, strain the stock.

5. Remove the jars from the canner, empty into the sink, and place them on a cutting board on a nearby countertop.

6. Ladle the hot stock into the prepared jars, leaving 1 inch of headspace. Use a nonmetallic utensil to release any air bubbles. Wipe the rims clean and seal with the lids and rings.

7. Put the jars on a rack in the pressure canner. Lock the lid in place, bring to a boil, and let the canner vent for 10 minutes. Put the weighted gauge or pressure regulator on the vent.

8. Process for 20 minutes at 11 pounds on a dial gauge or at 10 pounds on a weighted gauge. Adjust the pressure as necessary based on your altitude (see page 233). Adjust the temperature to maintain an even pressure. Turn off the heat. Let the pressure drop to zero before opening the lid.

9. Carefully remove the jars from the canner. Set aside to cool, undisturbed, for 12 hours.

10. Check the lids for proper seals (see page 32). Remove the rings, wipe the jars, label and date them, and transfer to a cupboard or pantry.

11. Refrigerate any jars that don't seal properly, and use within 5 days. Properly sealed jars will last in the cupboard for 12 months. Once opened, refrigerate and consume within 5 days.

PAIR IT

Vegetable stock can be used in countless ways to add flavor and nutrition to meals. Swap it for cooking water for more flavorful rice, or use it as a base for a vegetarian gravy. Once you open a jar, freeze any unused portion in an ice cube tray or muffin tin to extend its useful life and have ready-measured portions anytime you need them.

8

PICKLED FOODS

The acidic crunch of pickles makes the process of canning so worth the effort. Using simple vinegar and salt brines, you can turn your favorite produce into lasting pickled products with simple recipes that span the garden's bounty. From mouth-puckeringly sour to perfectly sweet pickles, there is something to satisfy everyone's unique taste buds in the wide world of pickled foods.

BREAD-AND-BUTTER PICKLES

MAKES 8 PINT JARS

WATER-BATH CANNING

These sweet, mild pickles are a hands-down favorite for eating from the jar or adding to sandwiches. If you have a ripple-bladed cutter, use it for extra visual appeal. No matter how you slice them, aim for fairly even pieces about the same thickness.

PREP TIME: 20 minutes, plus 4 hours cooling time
COOK TIME: 5 minutes
PROCESSING TIME: 10 minutes
TOTAL TIME: 4 hours, 35 minutes

6 pounds pickling cucumbers, cut into ¼-inch-thick slices
2 yellow onions, cut into ¼-inch-thick slices
¼ cup kosher salt
3 cups cracked ice
2 cups apple cider vinegar
2 cups sugar
1 tablespoon yellow mustard seed
½ teaspoon celery seed
½ teaspoon ground turmeric

1. In a large bowl, combine the cucumbers and onions. Sprinkle evenly with the kosher salt. Toss to combine.

2. Cover the vegetables with a clean, flat-weave kitchen towel. Top with a 2-inch-thick layer of ice. Refrigerate for 3 to 4 hours.

3. Transfer the cucumbers and onions to a colander. Rinse thoroughly and drain.

4. Prepare a hot water bath (see page 30). Place the jars in it to keep warm. Wash the lids and rings in hot, soapy water, and set aside.

5. In a large saucepot set over high heat, combine the vinegar, sugar, mustard seed, celery seed, and turmeric. Bring to a boil.

6. Add the cucumbers and onions. Return to a simmer. Cook for 5 minutes.

7. With a slotted spoon, transfer the cucumbers and onions to the prepared jars, leaving 1 inch of headspace

8. Ladle the hot vinegar brine over, making sure the pickles are submerged and leaving ½ inch of headspace. Use a nonmetallic utensil to release any air bubbles. Wipe the rims clean and seal with the lids and rings.

9. Process the jars in a hot water bath (see page 31) for 10 minutes. Turn off the heat and let the jars rest in the water bath for 10 minutes.

10. Carefully remove the jars from the hot water canner. Set aside to cool for 12 hours.

11. Check the lids for proper seals (see page 32). Remove the rings, wipe the jars, label and date them, and transfer to a cupboard or pantry.

12. For the best flavor, let the pickles rest for at least 2 to 3 weeks before serving. Refrigerate any jars that don't seal properly, and use within 2 months. Properly sealed jars will last in the cupboard for 12 months. Once opened, refrigerate and consume within 2 months.

TRY INSTEAD

You can substitute zucchini or summer squash for the cucumbers. Look for ones that are 2 to 2½ inches in diameter.

ICICLE PICKLES

MAKES 5 PINT JARS

WATER-BATH CANNING

This pickle takes 14 days to get ready for canning, but it isn't two weeks of constant work—and it's worth the wait. The long fermentation period creates an unusual pickle that is sweet and tart with a crisp texture. Because these pickles rest at room temperature, it is important to be very clean as you work. Wash your pickling container or crock and the plate used as a weight with plenty of warm, soapy water in between soakings and rinse with the hottest water possible.

PREP TIME: 20 minutes, plus 14 days fermenting time
COOK TIME: 1 hour
PROCESSING TIME: 10 minutes
TOTAL TIME: 14 days, 1 hour, 30 minutes

- 6 pounds unwaxed pickling cucumbers, rinsed, blossom ends trimmed
- 3/4 cup pickling salt, divided
- 6 quarts cold water, divided
- 1 tablespoon pickling spices
- 2 teaspoons celery seed
- 4 cups white vinegar
- 5 1/2 cups sugar, divided

DAYS 1 TO 2

1. To a large container or crock, add the cucumbers.
2. In a large saucepan set over high heat, combine 1/4 cup of pickling salt with 2 quarts of cold water. Bring to a boil. Pour the hot liquid over the cucumbers. Top with a clean plate as a weight to submerge them. Cover and rest at room temperature for 2 days.

DAYS 3 TO 6

1. On Days 3 and 5, drain the cucumbers and rinse well. Thoroughly wash and dry the container and the plate. Add the cucumbers back to the container.
2. Repeat step 2 from Day 1.

DAY 7

1. Drain the pickles. Cut them into slices, chunks, or spears. Thoroughly clean and dry the container and the plate.
2. In a cheesecloth square, combine the pickling spices and celery seed. Tie securely with kitchen twine into a sachet.

3. In a large saucepan set over medium-high heat, combine the vinegar, 2 cups of sugar, and the sachet. Bring to a simmer. Cook for 1 to 2 minutes, or until the sugar dissolves.

4. Return the cucumbers to the container. Pour the hot syrup over the cucumbers. Cover with the plate to submerge them and rest overnight.

DAYS 8 TO 13

1. In a medium saucepan over medium-high heat, strain the pickle syrup, reserving the sachet.

2. Thoroughly wash and dry the container and plate. Return the pickles to the container.

3. Add the reserved sachet and ½ cup of sugar to the syrup. Bring to a boil. Pour the liquid over the pickles, weight with the plate, and rest for 1 day.

4. Repeat steps 1 to 3 for days 9 to 13

DAY 14

1. Prepare a hot water bath (see page 30). Place the jars in it to keep warm. Wash the lids and rings in hot, soapy water, and set aside.

2. Over a saucepan, strain the pickles, catching the syrup in the pan. Discard the sachet.

3. Fill the prepared jars with the pickles, leaving ½ inch of headspace.

4. Stir the remaining ½ cup of sugar into the syrup. Bring to a boil.

5. Ladle the hot syrup over the pickles, leaving ½ inch of headspace. Use a nonmetallic utensil to release any air bubbles. Wipe the rims clean and seal with the lids and rings.

6. Process the jars in a hot water bath (see page 31) for 10 minutes. Turn off the heat and let the jars rest in the water bath for 10 minutes.

7. Carefully remove the jars from the hot water canner. Set aside to cool for 12 hours.

8. Check the lids for proper seals (see page 32). Remove the rings, wipe the jars, label and date them, and transfer to a cupboard or pantry.

9. For the best flavor, let the pickles rest for 2 to 3 weeks before serving. Refrigerate any jars that don't seal properly, and use within 2 months. Properly sealed jars will last in the cupboard for 12 months. Once opened, refrigerate and consume within 2 months.

CLOSER LOOK

Unlike typical store-bought cucumbers, pickling cucumbers often come with their blossom ends still attached. It is thought that leaving this end on leads to softening and spoilage of pickles when canned. For this reason, it is always removed. Either scrape or cut it off before using pickling cucumbers.

CORNICHONS

MAKES 4 PINT JARS

WATER-BATH CANNING

These tiny whole pickles look like sweet baby gherkins. They have a sharp bite and a crisp snap that is nearly the polar opposite, though. True cornichons are made from a specific variety of French cucumber, but any very small cucumber variety, picked while no more than 2 inches long, will yield similar results.

PREP TIME: 10 minutes, plus 3 to 4 hours resting time
COOK TIME: 5 minutes
PROCESSING TIME: 15 minutes
TOTAL TIME: 4 hours, 30 minutes

- 3 pounds small pickling cucumbers, blossom ends trimmed
- ½ cup kosher salt
- 4 fresh tarragon sprigs, divided
- 4 garlic cloves, peeled, divided
- 4 cups white wine vinegar
- 4 whole cloves
- 4 bay leaves
- 2 teaspoons black peppercorns
- 2 teaspoons white peppercorns

1. In a colander set in the sink or over a large bowl, combine the cucumbers and kosher salt. Let stand for 3 to 4 hours to release their juices.

2. Rinse the cucumbers well and drain them.

3. Prepare a hot water bath (see page 30). Place the jars in it to keep warm. Wash the lids and rings in hot, soapy water, and set aside.

4. To each jar, add 1 sprig of tarragon and 1 garlic clove.

5. Fill the jars with the cucumbers, packing them as snugly as possible, leaving ½ inch of headspace.

6. In a small saucepan set over medium-high heat, combine the white vinegar, cloves, bay leaves, black peppercorns, and white peppercorns. Bring to a boil.

7. Pour the liquid over the cucumbers, covering completely, leaving ½ inch of headspace. Use a nonmetallic utensil to release any air bubbles. Wipe the rims clean and seal with the lids and rings.

8. Process the jars in a hot water bath (see page 31) for 15 minutes. Turn off the heat and let the jars rest in the water bath for 10 minutes.

9. Carefully remove the jars from the hot water canner. Set aside to cool for 12 hours.

10. Check the lids for proper seals (see page 32). Remove the rings, wipe the jars, label and date them, and transfer to a cupboard or pantry.

11. For the best flavor, let the pickles rest for at least 2 to 3 weeks before serving. Refrigerate any jars that don't seal properly, and use within 2 months. Properly sealed jars will last in the cupboard for 12 months. Once opened, refrigerate and consume within 2 months.

CLOSER LOOK

Cornichons are a particularly delicate type of cucumber and should be processed immediately upon picking, but will typically last for 1 to 2 days. For all other pickling cucumbers, process within 3 days. If you can't pickle cucumbers immediately, store them in a cool spot such as a basement. Do not store them in the refrigerator, as this can dry them out.

DILLY BEANS

MAKES 5 PINT JARS

WATER-BATH CANNING

These tart pickled beans are easy to make and are always a nice gift to send home with visitors or share as a thank-you present. Fresh dill sprigs, if available, are a lovely way to flavor these pickled beans. Substitute one or two fresh sprigs for each teaspoon of dill seed.

PREP TIME: 15 minutes
COOK TIME: 5 minutes
PROCESSING TIME: 10 minutes
TOTAL TIME: 30 minutes

5 garlic cloves, divided
5 teaspoons dill seed, divided
2½ teaspoons peppercorns, divided
3 pounds green beans, rinsed, stemmed, and cut to fit the canning jars
2½ cups white vinegar
2½ cups water
4 tablespoons pickling salt

1. Prepare a hot water bath (see page 30). Place the jars in it to keep warm. Wash the lids and rings in hot, soapy water, and set aside.

2. To each jar, add 1 garlic clove, 1 teaspoon of dill seed, and ½ teaspoon of peppercorns.

3. Pack the beans into the jars so they stand up.

4. In a medium saucepan set over medium heat, combine the vinegar, water, and pickling salt. Bring to a boil.

5. Pour the brine into the jars covering the beans completely, leaving ½ inch of headspace. Use a non-metallic utensil to release any air bubbles. Wipe the rims clean and seal with the lids and rings.

6. Process the jars in a hot water bath (see page 31) for 10 minutes. Turn off the heat and let the jars rest in the water bath for 10 minutes.

7. Carefully remove the jars from the hot water canner. Set aside to cool for 12 hours.

8. Check the lids for proper seals (see page 32). Remove the rings, wipe the jars, label and date them, and transfer to a cupboard or pantry.

9. For the best flavor, let the pickles rest for 2 to 3 weeks before serving. Refrigerate any jars that don't seal properly, and use within 2 months. Properly sealed jars will last in the cupboard for 12 months. Once opened, refrigerate and consume within 2 months.

TRY INSTEAD

If you don't care for dill, or don't have any on hand, try other herbs with these beans. Basil, tarragon, and rosemary all combine well with the snap and sour of a pickled bean.

WATERMELON PICKLES

MAKES 5 PINT JARS

WATER-BATH CANNING

This pickle is a sweet, hot, sour burst of flavor. It's a true Southern classic, typically served with cheese and crackers. It can also be served with sandwiches or added to salads for some zing. Use the red flesh for juice, fruit salad, or freeze it for easy homemade ice pops.

PREP TIME: 4 hours, 30 minutes, plus overnight chilling time
COOK TIME: 1 hour, 15 minutes
PROCESSING TIME: 10 minutes
TOTAL TIME: 5 hours, 55 minutes, plus overnight chilling time

1 (6-pound) watermelon
¾ cup salt
3 quarts plus 3 cups water
2 quarts ice cubes
2 cinnamon sticks, broken into 1-inch pieces
1 teaspoon whole cloves
9 cups sugar
3 cups white vinegar
1 lemon, seeded and thinly sliced

DAY 1

1. Cut open the watermelon. Trim the red flesh from the rind and reserve it for another use.

2. With a vegetable peeler, peel away the dark green outer skin of the rind and discard. Cut the rind into 1-inch squares or fancy shapes, as desired. You should have about 10 cups. Add it to a container large enough to hold with the brine.

3. In a large pot, stir together the salt and 3 quarts of water. Pour it over the rind. Top with the ice. Let stand for 4 hours.

4. In a colander, drain the rind. Rinse well with cold water.

5. Transfer the rind to a deep pot set over medium-high heat. Add enough cold water to cover by 1 inch. Bring to a simmer. Cook for about 10 minutes, or until fork-tender. Drain the rind and return it to the container.

6. In a cheesecloth square, combine the cinnamon sticks and cloves. Tie securely with kitchen twine into a sachet.

7. In a medium saucepan set over high heat, combine the sugar, white vinegar, remaining 3 cups of water, and the sachet. Bring to a boil, stirring to dissolve the sugar. Boil for 5 minutes. Pour the hot syrup, with the sachet, over the watermelon rind. Add the lemon slices. Cover and refrigerate overnight.

Continued

WATERMELON PICKLES

CONTINUED

DAY 2

1. To a preserving pot set over medium-high heat, transfer the rind and syrup. Bring to a boil. Reduce the heat to low. Simmer for 1 hour, stirring frequently, or until the syrup is thick and the pickles are very tender.

2. Prepare a hot water bath (see page 30). Place the jars in it to keep warm. Wash the lids and rings in hot, soapy water, and set aside.

3. Open the sachet, and transfer a small piece of cinnamon stick into each jar. Discard the cloves.

4. Using a slotted spoon, transfer the pickles into the prepared jars. Ladle the syrup over, leaving ¼ inch of headspace. Use a nonmetallic utensil to release any air bubbles in the syrup. Wipe the rims clean and seal with the lids and rings.

5. Process the jars in a hot water bath (see page 31) for 10 minutes. Turn off the heat and let the jars rest in the water bath for 10 minutes.

6. Carefully remove the jars from the hot water canner. Set aside to cool for 12 hours.

7. Check the lids for proper seals (see page 32). Remove the rings, wipe the jars, label and date them, and transfer to a cupboard or pantry.

8. Refrigerate any jars that don't seal properly, and use within 3 weeks. Properly sealed jars will last in the cupboard for 12 months. Once opened, refrigerate and consume within 3 weeks.

PICKLED BEETS

MAKES 4 PINT JARS, OR 2 QUART JARS

WATER-BATH CANNING

The beets in this recipe are fully cooked before a vinegar brine is added to give them the wonderful and unforgettable texture of pickled beets. You can pickle any variety of beet, including golden and rainbow varieties. You can pack together different types, but adding the standard red beet to any lighter-flesh ones will color the entire jar magenta.

PREP TIME: 15 minutes
COOK TIME: 35 minutes
PROCESSING TIME: 30 minutes
TOTAL TIME: 1 hour, 20 minutes

- 7 pounds beets, stem and root ends trimmed
- 2 cinnamon sticks
- 12 whole cloves
- 4 cups white vinegar
- 2 cups sugar
- 2 cups water
- 1½ teaspoons canning or pickling salt
- 4 yellow onions, cut into ½-inch rounds or matchsticks (optional)

1. Prepare a hot water bath (see page 30). Place the jars in it to keep warm. Wash the lids and rings in hot, soapy water, and set aside.

2. In a large pot set over high heat, combine the beets and enough cold water to cover completely. Bring to a boil. Reduce the heat to medium. Continue to boil for 20 to 30 minutes, or until tender enough to pierce easily with a wooden skewer or the tip of a paring knife.

3. Drain the beets in a colander and cool. Pull or cut away the skins. Cut into desired shapes.

4. In a cheesecloth square, combine the cinnamon and cloves. Tie securely with kitchen twine into a sachet.

5. In a large saucepot set over high heat, combine the white vinegar, sugar, water, canning salt, and the sachet. Bring to a boil.

6. Add the beets and onions (if using). Return to a simmer for 5 minutes. Remove and discard the sachet.

7. With a slotted spoon, transfer the beets and onions to the jars, leaving ½ inch of headspace. Ladle the hot vinegar mixture over, leaving ½ inch of headspace. Use a nonmetallic utensil to release any air bubbles. Wipe the rims clean and seal with the lids and rings.

Continued

PICKLED BEETS
CONTINUED

8. Process the jars in a hot water bath (see page 31) for 30 minutes. Turn off the heat and let the jars rest in the water bath for 10 minutes.

9. Carefully remove the jars from the hot water canner. Set aside to cool for 12 hours.

10. Check the lids for proper seals (see page 32). Remove the rings, wipe the jars, label and date them, and transfer the jars to a cupboard or pantry.

11. For the best flavor, let the beets rest for 2 to 3 weeks before serving. Refrigerate any jars that don't seal properly, and use within 2 months. Properly sealed jars will last in the cupboard for 12 months. Once opened, refrigerate and consume within 2 months.

PREPARATION TIP

Beets can stain your hands. Wear kitchen gloves while working with them to prevent this. Cut large beets into slices or sticks. Smaller beets and baby beets can be left whole, or cut in halves or wedges.

PICKLED JALAPEÑOS

MAKES 6 PINT JARS

WATER-BATH CANNING

Use any hot pepper you like for this pickle, or a combination if you prefer. The best results come from chiles that are somewhat fleshy, like jalapeños, banana, Hungarian, and Cubanelles. Unlike some recipes for pickled peppers, this one does not require an initial peeling. If you prefer, instead of cutting the peppers into rings, you can simply make a few slits in small chiles and leave them whole.

PREP TIME: 3 hours, 30 minutes, plus 18 hours curing time
COOK TIME: 5 minutes
PROCESSING TIME: 30 minutes
TOTAL TIME: 22 hours, 5 minutes

- 1½ gallons water
- 1½ cups pickling lime
- 3 pounds jalapeño peppers, or other chiles, sliced ¼ inch thick
- 7½ cups apple cider vinegar
- 1¾ cups water
- 2½ tablespoons canning salt
- 6 tablespoons yellow mustard seed, divided
- 3 tablespoons celery seed, divided

DAY 1

Fill a large container with the water and carefully stir in the pickling lime. Add the peppers. Refrigerate for 18 hours.

DAY 2

1. In a colander, drain and rinse the peppers under cold running water. Rinse the container, return the peppers to it, and cover with cold water. Refrigerate for 1 hour.

2. Repeat step 1 twice more, for a total of three fresh water soakings.

3. Prepare a hot water bath (see page 30). Place the jars in it to keep warm. Wash the lids and rings in hot, soapy water, and set aside.

4. In a large saucepot set over high heat, combine the cider vinegar, water, and canning salt. Bring to a boil.

5. Into each jar, add 1 tablespoon of mustard seed and 1½ teaspoons of celery seed. Fill the jars with the peppers, leaving ½ inch of headspace. Ladle the hot vinegar brine over, leaving ½ inch of headspace. Use a nonmetallic utensil to release any air bubbles. Wipe the rims clean and seal with the lids and rings.

6. Process the jars in a hot water bath (see page 31) for 30 minutes. Turn off the heat and let the jars rest in the water bath for 10 minutes.

Continued

PICKLED JALAPEÑOS

CONTINUED

7. Carefully remove the jars from the hot water canner. Set aside to cool for 12 hours.

8. Check the lids for proper seals (see page 32). Remove the rings, wipe the jars, label, and transfer the jars to a cupboard or pantry.

9. For the best flavor, let the pickles rest for 2 to 3 weeks before serving. Refrigerate any jars that don't seal properly, and use within 2 months. Properly sealed jars will last in the cupboard for 12 months. Once opened, refrigerate and consume within 2 months.

PREPARATION TIP

When preparing a large amount of hot peppers for canning, it is important that you cover your hands with kitchen gloves to prevent burns. While you may not notice any effect when cutting one or two peppers, a large amount can cause significant irritation. Also, don't touch your eyes or nose while cutting these peppers, and wash your hands thoroughly when finished.

PICKLED ONIONS

MAKES 6 PINT JARS

WATER-BATH CANNING

These delicious pickled onions give you bragging rights next time you make Gibsons or martinis at home. They can also be chopped into egg, pasta, or potato salads for a tangy bite. This recipe works with any small round onion about the size of a large marble, including pearl onions, boiling onions, pickling onions, and red or white cippolini onions.

PREP TIME: 5 minutes
COOK TIME: 10 minutes
PROCESSING TIME: 10 minutes
TOTAL TIME: 25 minutes

8 cups pearl onions
12 teaspoons mustard seed, divided
6 teaspoons celery seed, divided
5½ cups white vinegar
2 cups sugar
1 cup water
2 teaspoons canning salt

1. Bring a large pot of water to a rolling boil. Add the onions. Boil for about 2 minutes, or just long enough to loosen the skins. Drain in a colander and cool. When cool enough to handle, slice the ends from the onions and pop them out of their skins.

2. Prepare a hot water bath (see page 30). Place the jars in it to keep warm. Wash the lids and rings in hot, soapy water, and set aside.

3. Into each jar, add 2 teaspoons of mustard seed and 1 teaspoon of celery seed.

4. In a large saucepot set over high heat, combine the white vinegar, sugar, water, and canning salt. Bring to a boil.

5. Add the onions. Return to a simmer. Cook for about 5 minutes, or until about half cooked.

6. With a slotted spoon, transfer the onions to the prepared jars, leaving ½ inch of headspace. Ladle the hot brine over, leaving ½ inch of headspace. Use a nonmetallic utensil to release any air bubbles. Wipe the rims clean and seal with the lids and rings.

7. Process the jars in a hot water bath (see page 31) for 10 minutes. Turn off the heat and let the jars rest in the water bath for 10 minutes.

8. Carefully remove the jars from the hot water canner. Set aside to cool for 12 hours.

9. Check the lids for proper seals (see page 32). Remove the rings, wipe the jars, label and date them, and transfer to a cupboard or pantry.

10. For the best flavor, let the pickles rest for at least 2 to 3 weeks before serving. Refrigerate any jars that don't seal properly, and use within 2 months. Properly sealed jars will last in the cupboard for 12 months. Once opened, refrigerate and consume within 2 months.

GARLIC CARROTS

MAKES 6 PINT JARS

WATER-BATH CANNING

These spicy, garlicky carrots are the perfect topping for grilled fish or burgers. You can add them to coleslaw and other salads for a kick of heat. Use any carrots you have available, including red, purple, and yellow varieties.

PREP TIME: 20 minutes
COOK TIME: 5 minutes
PROCESSING TIME: 10 minutes
TOTAL TIME: 35 minutes

12 whole cloves
1½ teaspoons red pepper flakes
6 garlic cloves, peeled and crushed
5 pounds carrots, ends removed, peeled, and cut into ½-inch-thick sticks
5 cups white vinegar
2 cups apple cider vinegar
1⅔ cups granulated sugar
5 tablespoons pickling salt

1. Prepare a hot water bath (see page 30). Place the jars in it to keep warm. Wash the lids and rings in hot, soapy water, and set aside.

2. Into each jar, add 2 cloves, ¼ teaspoon red pepper flakes, and 1 garlic clove.

3. Pack the carrots into the jars so they stand up.

4. In a large saucepan set over medium heat, combine the white vinegar, cider vinegar, sugar, and pickling salt. Bring to a boil.

5. Pour the brine into the jars, covering the carrots completely, leaving ½ inch of headspace. Use a non-metallic utensil to release any air bubbles. Wipe the rims clean and seal with the lids and rings.

6. Process the jars in a hot water bath (see page 31) for 10 minutes. Turn off the heat and let the jars rest in the water bath for 10 minutes.

7. Carefully remove the jars from the hot water canner. Set aside to cool for 12 hours.

8. Check the lids for proper seals (see page 32). Remove the rings, wipe the jars, label and date them, and transfer to a cupboard or pantry.

9. For the best flavor, let the pickles rest for at least 1 to 2 weeks before serving. Refrigerate any jars that don't seal properly, and use within 2 months. Properly sealed jars will last in the cupboard for 12 months. Once opened, refrigerate and consume within 2 months.

GIARDINIERA

MAKES 6 PINT JARS

WATER-BATH CANNING

The trick to a beautiful and delicious giardiniera is selecting picture-perfect produce. You can vary the vegetable combinations to suit your preferences and add more, or hotter, chiles to satisfy your heat preference. Enjoy this giardiniera as part of a pickle plate or tuck it into sandwiches made with hearty sausages and cured meats.

PREP TIME: 20 minutes
COOK TIME: 5 minutes
PROCESSING TIME: 10 minutes
TOTAL TIME: 35 minutes

- 1 cauliflower head, cut into florets
- 4 bell peppers, seeded and cut into wedges or strips
- 4 carrots, peeled and sliced
- 4 celery stalks, cut into 2-inch pieces
- 6 bay leaves, divided
- 6 fresh oregano sprigs, divided
- 18 garlic cloves, divided
- 1 tablespoon peppercorns, divided
- 6 tablespoons extra-virgin olive oil, divided
- 3 cups white wine vinegar
- 1 ½ cups water
- 1 teaspoon salt

1. Prepare a hot water bath (see page 30). Place the jars in it to keep warm. Wash the lids and rings in hot, soapy water, and set aside.

2. Evenly divide the cauliflower, bell peppers, carrots, and celery among the prepared jars.

3. Into each jar, tuck in 1 bay leaf, 1 oregano sprig, 3 garlic cloves, and ½ teaspoon of peppercorns.

4. Spoon 1 tablespoon of olive oil into each jar.

5. In a medium saucepot set over high heat, combine the white wine vinegar, water, and salt. Bring to a boil. Ladle the brine over the vegetables, leaving ½ inch of headspace. Use a nonmetallic utensil to release any air bubbles. Wipe the rims clean and seal with the lids and rings.

6. Process the jars in a hot water bath (see page 31) for 10 minutes. Turn off the heat and let the jars rest in the water bath for 10 minutes.

7. Carefully remove the jars from the hot water canner. Set aside to cool for 12 hours.

8. Check the lids for proper seals (see page 32). Remove the rings, wipe the jars, label and date them, and transfer to a cupboard or pantry.

9. Refrigerate any jars that don't seal properly, and use within 2 months. Properly sealed jars will last in the cupboard for 12 months. Once opened, refrigerate and consume within 2 months.

PICKLED COLLARD GREENS

MAKES 5 PINT JARS

WATER-BATH CANNING, LOW-SODIUM

With so many options for pickled produce, pickling greens may not have crossed your mind. If you have never tried them, here's your chance! These simple, slightly spicy greens work well on a sandwich or cooked into a coconut milk curry. Or if you like, they can be served as a side.

PREP TIME: 15 minutes
COOK TIME: 5 minutes
PROCESSING TIME: 15 minutes
TOTAL TIME: 35 minutes

- 3 pounds collard greens
- 2 tablespoons mustard seed
- 2 teaspoons cardamom pods, gently crushed
- 5 cups apple cider vinegar
- ½ cup balsamic vinegar
- ¾ cup water
- 1½ tablespoons salt
- 1 tablespoon sugar
- 5 serrano chiles, divided
- 5 garlic cloves, peeled, divided
- 5 shallots, peeled, divided

1. Prepare a hot water bath (see page 30). Place the jars in it to keep warm. Wash the lids and rings in hot, soapy water, and set aside.

2. Wash the greens well, changing the water several times. Remove and discard the thick ribs or save for Vegetable Stock (see page 180), Chicken or Turkey Stock (see page 206), or Beef Stock (see page 208).

3. Stack the collard greens and slice them crosswise into strips about ¾ inch thick. Use a salad spinner to remove excess water. If you do not have a salad spinner, place the greens in a clean pillowcase and shake vigorously.

4. In a small bowl, combine the mustard seed and cardamom pods.

5. In a medium saucepot set over high heat, combine the apple cider vinegar, balsamic vinegar, water, salt, and sugar. Bring to a boil.

6. Pack the greens into the prepared jars as tightly as possible.

7. To each jar, add 1 chile, 1 garlic clove, and 1 shallot. Evenly divide the spices (about 1⅓ teaspoons each) among the jars. Ladle the brine over the vegetables, leaving ½ inch of headspace. Use a nonmetallic utensil to release any air bubbles. Wipe the rims clean and seal with the lids and rings.

8. Process the jars in a hot water bath (see page 31) for 15 minutes. Turn off the heat and let the jars rest in the water bath for 10 minutes.

9. Carefully remove the jars from the hot water canner. Set aside to cool for 12 hours.

10. Check the lids for proper seals (see page 32). Remove the rings, wipe the jars, label and date them, and transfer to a cupboard or pantry.

11. Refrigerate any jars that don't seal properly, and use within 2 months. Properly sealed jars will last in the cupboard for 12 months. Once opened, refrigerate and consume within 2 months.

TRY INSTEAD

If you don't like, or don't have, collards, try this recipe with any other sturdy green. Kale, mustard greens, or turnip greens have a similar flavor. With all of these, wash them very thoroughly as they grow close to the ground and tend to be quite dirty.

ARTICHOKE HEARTS IN OIL

MAKES 4 PINT JARS

WATER-BATH CANNING

You'll prepare the artichokes in this recipe to remove as much moisture as possible so the oil and seasonings can permeate completely. As the artichokes rest in the jars, air bubbles may rise to the surface and the level of the oil may drop. Top it off whenever necessary to keep the artichokes completely submerged. If you can, use baby artichokes. Simply trim the stems, snip the barbs from the leaves, and cut into halves or quarters. Use a spoon to scrape out the feathery choke.

PREP TIME: 30 minutes
COOK TIME: 20 minutes, plus 2 to 3 hours for draining time
PROCESSING TIME: 15 minutes
TOTAL TIME: 4 hours, 5 minutes

1 cup freshly squeezed lemon juice, divided
2 bay leaves
4 teaspoons salt, divided
2 lemons, halved
4 pounds artichokes
2 cups white vinegar
1 cup extra-virgin olive oil
4 garlic cloves, finely chopped
4 dried chiles
12 juniper berries (optional)

1. Fill a large pot about halfway with water. Add ½ cup of lemon juice, the bay leaves, and 2 teaspoons of salt.

2. Working with one artichoke at a time, cut away the stem and trim the outer leaves, keeping the tender inner leaves. Cut in half. With a spoon, scoop out the feathery choke. Rub all cut surfaces with the lemon halves and immediately drop into the pot. Continue until all are trimmed.

3. Place the pot over medium-high heat. Bring to a simmer. Cook for about 15 minutes, or until the artichokes pierce easily with the tip of a paring knife. Drain well in a colander.

4. Arrange the artichokes on a few layers of clean linen towels (not terry). Top with a few more layers. Press down on the artichokes lightly. Let them drain for 2 or 3 hours to remove as much liquid as possible.

5. Prepare a hot water bath (see page 30). Place the jars in it to keep warm. Wash the lids and rings in hot, soapy water, and set aside.

6. In a medium saucepot set over medium-high heat, combine the white vinegar with the remaining ½ cup of lemon juice, the remaining 2 teaspoons of salt, the olive oil, garlic, chiles, and juniper berries (if using). Bring to a boil.

7. Pack the artichokes into the prepared jars. Ladle the hot vinegar-oil mixture over, completely covering the artichokes, leaving ½ inch of headspace. Push down on the artichokes with a nonmetallic utensil to release any air pockets. The artichokes should still be completely covered. Wipe the rims clean and seal with the lids and rings.

8. Process the jars in a hot water bath (see page 31) for 15 minutes. Turn off the heat and let the jars rest in the water bath for 10 minutes.

9. Carefully remove the jars from the hot water canner. Set aside to cool for 12 hours.

10. Check the lids for proper seals (see page 32). Remove the rings, wipe the jars, label and date them, and transfer the jars to a cupboard or pantry.

11. For the best flavor, let the artichokes rest for 2 to 3 weeks before serving. Refrigerate any jars that don't seal properly, and use within 2 months. Properly sealed jars will last in the cupboard for 12 months. Once opened, refrigerate and consume within 2 months.

DID YOU KNOW?

You may have heard that processing foods with oil in a hot water-bath is not safe. That would be true if it was just oil, but this recipe includes a healthy dose of acid, and that makes it safe for processing. Be very careful to wipe the jar rims clean, however, because even a trace of oil can prevent a good seal from forming.

9

CANNED SOUPS, STEWS, MEATS & MORE

Canning soups, stews, and meats gives you a ready-made fast food depository to keep all year long. Preserve your favorites and have multiple quick choices for mealtime at your fingertips. Once you get started, it is hard to stop putting up food for busy nights so you can eat healthy even when life gets in the way. The recipes in this chapter all require a pressure canner.

CHICKEN OR TURKEY STOCK

MAKES 4 QUART JARS, 8 PINT JARS, OR A COMBINATION

PRESSURE CANNING

Homemade turkey and chicken stocks are made with the picked-over carcass of the respective bird—something you might otherwise throw away. You'll never buy packaged stocks again once you get the hang of making this simple blend in your pressure canner. Not only will you cut your sodium intake, but you will also create more flavorful soups and stews using this recipe.

PREP TIME: 5 minutes
COOK TIME: 2 to 3 hours
PROCESSING TIME: 20 to 25 minutes
TOTAL TIME: 3 hours, 30 minutes

1 chicken, or turkey, carcass
3 celery stalks
1 large onion
3 carrots
1 bunch fresh parsley
1 tablespoon peppercorns
2 tablespoons white vinegar
8 quarts water
4 teaspoons salt, divided (optional)

1. In a large stockpot set over medium-high heat, combine the carcass, celery, onion, carrots, parsley, peppercorns, white vinegar, and water. Bring to a boil. Skim off any foam. Reduce the heat to low. Cover and simmer for 2 to 3 hours.

2. Prepare the jars, lids, and rings by washing them in hot, soapy water.

3. Place a rack in a pressure canner and add 3 to 4 inches of water. Fill the jars with a couple inches of water so they do not float, and place them in the canner. Bring the water to a simmer until ready to fill the jars. *Do not boil the water.*

4. Remove the carcass from the pot and let it cool. When cool enough to handle, pick off any meat that remains and set aside.

5. With a wire mesh strainer, strain the stock and cool. Remove any fat. Return it to the pot and add the reserved meat. Bring to a boil.

6. Remove the jars from the canner, empty into the sink, and place them on a cutting board on a nearby countertop.

7. Filling one jar at a time, ladle in the stock, leaving 1 inch of headspace. Add 1 teaspoon of salt per quart jar, or ½ teaspoon of salt per pint jar (if using). Use a nonmetallic utensil to release any air bubbles. Wipe the rim clean and seal with the lid and ring. Put the jar on a rack in the pressure canner. Repeat until all jars are filled.

8. Lock the lid in place, bring to a boil, and let the canner vent for 10 minutes. Put the weighted gauge or pressure regulator on the vent.

9. Process quart jars for 25 minutes, or pint jars for 20 minutes at 11 pounds on a dial gauge or at 10 pounds on a weighted gauge. Adjust the pressure as necessary based on your altitude (see page 233). Adjust the temperature to maintain an even pressure. Turn off the heat. Let the pressure drop to zero before opening the lid.

10. Carefully remove the jars from the canner. Set aside to cool, undisturbed, for 12 hours.

11. Check the lids for proper seals (see page 32). Remove the rings, wipe the jars, label and date them, and transfer to a cupboard or pantry.

12. Refrigerate any jars that don't seal properly, and use within 5 days. Properly sealed jars will last in the cupboard for 12 months. Once opened, refrigerate and consume within 5 days.

LOW-SODIUM PREPARATION TIP

Depending on how you will use the stock, you may want to omit the salt. If you will be making soup, salt adds flavor and creates a rich base for the final product. However, if using for other recipes, it is beneficial to omit the salt and add it to the finished dish for better control of your overall sodium intake.

PREPARATION TIP

If you have time, consider refrigerating the soup overnight before canning. This helps you remove the fat more easily from the stock. When completely chilled, the fat solidifies and you can simply spoon it away for a more fully defatted stock.

BEEF STOCK

MAKES 4 QUART JARS, 8 PINT JARS, OR A COMBINATION

PRESSURE CANNING

Beef stock creates a hearty base for soups, sauces, and gravies. Use leftover beef bones from several meals, or fresh bones for even more flavor. Look for beef bones labeled "soup bones" in the grocery store, or visit a butcher for the best selection of quality, gelatin-rich bones.

PREP TIME: 5 minutes
COOK TIME: 2 to 3 hours
PROCESSING TIME: 20 to 25 minutes
TOTAL TIME: 3 hours, 30 minutes

2 to 3 pounds meaty beef bones
2 to 3 cups vegetable scraps, carrots, celery, greens, herbs, onions, etc. (optional)
2 tablespoons white vinegar
8 quarts water
4 teaspoons salt, divided (optional)

1. In a large stockpot set over medium-high heat, combine the beef bones, vegetable scraps (if using), white vinegar, and water. Bring to a boil. Skim off any foam. Reduce the heat to low. Cover and simmer for 2 to 3 hours.

2. Prepare the jars, lids, and rings by washing them in hot, soapy water.

3. Place a rack in a pressure canner and add 3 to 4 inches of water. Fill the jars with a couple inches of water so they do not float, and place them in the canner. Bring the water to a simmer until ready to fill the jars. *Do not boil the water.*

4. Remove the beef bones from the pot and cool. When cool enough to handle, pick off any meat and set aside.

5. With a wire mesh strainer set over a large bowl, strain the stock and cool. Skim off any fat. Return it to the pot and add the reserved meat. Bring to a boil.

6. Remove the jars from the canner, empty into the sink, and place them on a cutting board on a nearby countertop.

7. Filling one jar at a time, ladle in the stock, leaving 1 inch of headspace. Add 1 teaspoon of salt per quart jar, or ½ teaspoon of salt per pint (if using). Use a nonmetallic utensil to release any air bubbles. Wipe the rim clean, and seal with the lid and ring. Put the jar on a rack in the pressure canner. Repeat until all jars are filled.

8. Lock the lid in place, bring to a boil, and let the canner vent for 10 minutes. Put the weighted gauge or pressure regulator on the vent.

9. Process quart jars for 25 minutes, or pint jars for 20 minutes at 11 pounds on a dial gauge or at 10 pounds on a weighted gauge. Adjust the pressure as necessary based on your altitude (see page 233). Adjust the temperature to maintain an even pressure. Turn off the heat. Let the pressure drop to zero before opening the lid.

10. Carefully remove the jars from the canner. Set aside to cool, undisturbed, for 12 hours.

11. Check the lids for proper seals (see page 32). Remove the rings, wipe the jars, label and date them, and transfer to a cupboard or pantry.

12. Refrigerate any jars that don't seal properly, and use within 5 days. Properly sealed jars will last in the cupboard for 12 months. Once opened, refrigerate and consume within 5 days.

LOW-SODIUM PREPARATION TIP

Beef stock can be made with or without added salt. When omitting the salt, it is a tasty idea to add additional herbs and spices such as garlic, ginger, star anise, cilantro, or clove to impart additional flavor and create a tasty standalone product.

PREPARATION TIP

If using a combination of jar sizes when making stock, process them all for the longest time needed for the largest jar. While this could cause a loss of quality in some products, like pickles where firmness is desired, it makes no difference with stock and ensures it is safely prepared.

CHICKEN SOUP

MAKES 5 QUART JARS, OR 10 PINT JARS

PRESSURE CANNING, LOW-SODIUM

One of the most comforting foods in American cooking is chicken soup. Skip the high-sodium, preservative-laden, store-bought version and take comfort in this simple no-nonsense version. Since noodles and rice cannot be safely canned, this soup includes a large amount of broth to allow for adding them later with little adjustment. When ready to eat, add a handful of noodles or rice to your soup as it simmers.

PREP TIME: 15 minutes
COOK TIME: 30 minutes
PROCESSING TIME: 1 hour, 15 minutes to 1 hour, 30 minutes
TOTAL TIME: 2 hours, 15 minutes

16 cups chicken broth
2 cups shredded, or diced, cooked chicken
1 cup diced celery
1 cup diced carrots
1 onion, diced
Salt, for seasoning
Freshly ground black pepper, for seasoning

1. Prepare the jars, lids, and rings by washing them in hot, soapy water.

2. Place a rack in a pressure canner and add 3 to 4 inches of water. Fill the jars with a couple inches of water so they do not float, and place them in the canner. Bring the water to a simmer until ready to fill the jars. *Do not boil the water.*

3. In a large stockpot set over medium-high heat, combine the chicken broth, chicken meat, celery, carrots, and onion. Bring to a boil. Reduce the heat to low and simmer for 30 minutes. Season with salt and pepper.

4. Remove the jars from the canner, empty into the sink, and place them on a cutting board on a nearby countertop.

5. Fill the prepared jars about half full with the soup's solids. Ladle in the broth, leaving 1 inch of headspace. Use a nonmetallic utensil to release any air bubbles. Wipe the rims clean and seal with the lids and rings.

6. Put the jars on a rack in the pressure canner. Lock the lid in place, bring to a boil, and let the canner vent for 10 minutes. Put the weighted gauge or pressure regulator on the vent.

7. Process quart jars for 1 hour, 30 minutes, or pint jars for 1 hour, 15 minutes at 11 pounds on a dial gauge or at 10 pounds on a weighted gauge. Adjust the pressure as necessary based on your altitude (see page 233). Adjust the temperature to maintain an even pressure. Turn off the heat. Let the pressure drop to zero before opening the lid.

8. Carefully remove the jars from the canner. Set aside to cool, undisturbed, for 12 hours.

9. Check the lids for proper seals (see page 32). Remove the rings, wipe the jars, label and date them, and transfer to a cupboard or pantry.

10. Refrigerate any jars that don't seal properly, and use within 3 days. Properly sealed jars will last in the cupboard for 12 months. Once opened, refrigerate and consume within 3 days.

PEA SOUP

MAKES 6 PINT JARS

PRESSURE CANNING

Minimal prep work is needed to get this easy pea soup just right. The rich flavor of the ham makes this classic soup a standout. Next time you cook a ham, cube and set aside a bit of meat so you can turn a little into a lot with this economical and hearty recipe.

PREP TIME: 15 minutes
COOK TIME: 1 hour, 20 minutes
PROCESSING TIME: 1 hour, 15 minutes
TOTAL TIME: 2 hours, 50 minutes

3 cups dried split peas
12 cups water
2 cups diced carrots
1 ½ cups chopped onion
1 ½ cups chopped ham
4 garlic cloves, chopped
1 bay leaf
½ teaspoon sage
Salt, for seasoning
Freshly ground black pepper, for seasoning

1. In a large pot set over medium-high heat, combine the split peas and water. Bring to a boil. Reduce the heat to low. Cover and simmer for 1 hour, or until tender. If you want a smooth soup, mash the peas with a potato masher.

2. Prepare the jars, lids, and rings by washing them in hot, soapy water.

3. Place a rack in a pressure canner and add 3 to 4 inches of water. Fill the jars with a couple inches of water so they do not float, and place them in the canner. Bring the water to a simmer until ready to fill the jars. *Do not boil the water.*

4. To the peas, add the carrots, onion, ham, garlic, bay leaf, and sage. Season with salt and pepper. Bring to a simmer over medium heat. Cook for 20 minutes, stirring frequently.

5. Remove the jars from the canner, empty into the sink, and place them on a cutting board on a nearby countertop.

6. Ladle the soup into the prepared jars, leaving 1 inch of headspace. Use a nonmetallic utensil to release any air bubbles. Wipe the rims clean and seal with the lids and rings.

7. Put the jars on a rack in the pressure canner. Lock the lid in place, bring to a boil, and let the canner vent for 10 minutes. Put the weighted gauge or pressure regulator on the vent.

8. Process for 1 hour, 15 minutes at 11 pounds on a dial gauge or at 10 pounds on a weighted gauge. Adjust the pressure as necessary based on your altitude (see page 233). Adjust the temperature to maintain an even pressure. Turn off the heat. Let the pressure drop to zero before opening the lid.

9. Carefully remove the jars from the canner. Set aside to cool, undisturbed, for 12 hours.

10. Check the lids for proper seals (see page 32). Remove the rings, wipe the jars, label and date them, and transfer to a cupboard or pantry.

11. Refrigerate any jars that don't seal properly, and use within 3 days. Properly sealed jars will last in the cupboard for 12 months. Once opened, refrigerate and consume within 3 days.

PREPARATION TIP

If you prefer a creamy soup, use an immersion blender to quickly purée the soup. You can use a traditional blender, too, if you work in batches. Either way, be careful to avoid splashing the hot soup on your arms or face.

VEGETABLE SOUP

MAKES 8 PINT JARS

PRESSURE CANNING

Another classic comfort food, vegetable soup is a highly customizable treat that can be made to suit your individual taste. Substitute your favorite vegetables in the same ratios or add additional seasonings, as desired. When ready to eat, cook some noodles or rice and add them to the soup for a more filling meal.

PREP TIME: 20 minutes
COOK TIME: 15 minutes
PROCESSING TIME: 55 minutes
TOTAL TIME: 1 hour, 30 minutes

5 cups peeled and chopped tomatoes
3½ cups chopped potatoes
3½ cups sliced carrots
2 cups sweet peas
2 cups corn kernels
1 cup chopped celery
1 cup chopped onion
3½ cups chicken or vegetable broth, or water
Salt, for seasoning
Freshly ground black pepper, for seasoning

1. Prepare the jars, lids, and rings by washing them in hot, soapy water.

2. Place a rack in a pressure canner and add 3 to 4 inches of water. Fill the jars with a couple inches of water so they do not float, and place them in the canner. Bring the water to a simmer until ready to fill the jars. *Do not boil the water.*

3. In a large stockpot set over medium-high heat, combine the tomatoes, potatoes, carrots, peas, corn, celery, onion, and broth. Bring to a boil. Reduce the heat to low and simmer for 15 minutes, or until the tomatoes break down. Season with salt and pepper.

4. Remove the jars from the canner, empty into the sink, and place them on a cutting board on a nearby countertop.

5. Fill the prepared jars half full with the soup's solids. Ladle in the broth, leaving 1 inch of headspace. Use a nonmetallic utensil to release any air bubbles. Wipe the rims clean and seal with the lids and rings.

6. Put the jars on a rack in the pressure canner. Lock the lid in place, bring to a boil, and let the canner vent for 10 minutes. Put the weighted gauge or pressure regulator on the vent.

7. Process for 55 minutes at 11 pounds on a dial gauge or at 10 pounds on a weighted gauge. Adjust the pressure as necessary based on your altitude (see page 233). Adjust the temperature to maintain an even pressure. Turn off the heat. Let the pressure drop to zero before opening the lid.

8. Carefully remove the jars from the canner. Set aside to cool, undisturbed, for 12 hours.

9. Check the lids for proper seals (see page 32). Remove the rings, wipe the jars, label and date them, and transfer to a cupboard or pantry.

10. Refrigerate any jars that don't seal properly, and use within 3 days. Properly sealed jars will last in the cupboard for 12 months. Once opened, refrigerate and consume within 3 days.

BEEF AND VEGETABLE STEW

MAKES 4 QUART JARS, OR 8 PINT JARS

PRESSURE CANNING, LOW-SODIUM

Beef stew is a warming and welcoming meal on a cold day. Browning the meat before adding it to the stew ensures it is flavorful even after processing. Swap in any favorite vegetables in the same amounts called for here. Keep in mind, too, that each jar should be about half liquid and half solids.

PREP TIME: 20 minutes
COOK TIME: 20 minutes
PROCESSING TIME: 1 hour, 15 minutes to 1 hour, 30 minutes
TOTAL TIME: 2 hours, 10 minutes

2 pounds beef stew meat
1 ½ cups chopped onions
4 cups diced carrots
6 cups peeled, diced potatoes
8 cups beef broth
Salt, for seasoning
Freshly ground black pepper, for seasoning

1. Prepare the jars, lids, and rings by washing them in hot, soapy water.

2. Place a rack in a pressure canner and add 3 to 4 inches of water. Fill the jars with a couple inches of water so they do not float, and place them in the canner. Bring the water to a simmer until ready to fill the jars. *Do not boil the water.*

3. In a large pot set over medium-high heat, cook the beef for about 10 minutes, or until brown. Add the onion. Sauté for about 5 minutes, stirring regularly, or until softened and brown.

4. Add the carrots, potatoes, and beef broth. Season with salt and pepper. Bring to a boil.

5. Remove the jars from the canner, empty into the sink, and place them on a cutting board on a nearby countertop.

6. Fill the prepared jars about half full with the soup's solids. Ladle in the broth, leaving 1 inch of headspace. Use a nonmetallic utensil to release any air bubbles. Wipe the rims clean and seal with the lids and rings.

7. Put the jars on a rack in the pressure canner. Lock the lid in place, bring to a boil, and let the canner vent for 10 minutes. Put the weighted gauge or pressure regulator on the vent.

8. Process quart jars for 1 hour, 30 minutes, or pint jars for 1 hour, 15 minutes at 11 pounds on a dial gauge or at 10 pounds on a weighted gauge. Adjust the pressure as necessary based on your altitude (see page 233). Adjust the temperature to maintain an even pressure. Turn off the heat. Let the pressure drop to zero before opening the lid.

9. Carefully remove the jars from the canner. Set aside to cool, undisturbed, for 12 hours.

10. Check the lids for proper seals (see page 32). Remove the rings, wipe the jars, label and date them, and transfer to a cupboard or pantry.

11. Refrigerate any jars that don't seal properly, and use within 3 days. Properly sealed jars will last in the cupboard for 12 months. Once opened, refrigerate and consume within 3 days.

PREPARATION TIP

When canning soups and other items, thickening agents cannot be used, as they can impede the ability of the heat to penetrate and kill spores. However, it is quite easy to thicken a stew when preparing it to eat. Remove a cup of hot liquid from the stew. Mix in 1 to 2 tablespoons of cornstarch until smooth to create a slurry, stir this into the stew, and simmer briefly to thicken.

BEEF CHILI

MAKES 6 PINT JARS

PRESSURE CANNING

However you serve this rich beef chili—as a meal or to top a hot dog—it is delicious. Requiring minimal preparation and cooking time, this is a classic addition to any well-stocked pantry. Be sure to plan ahead for the overnight soaking of the beans to ensure a quality product. Adjust the peppers in the recipe to suit your taste for spice. For the really bold, use only hot chile peppers to create a super spicy dish.

PREP TIME: 15 minutes, plus overnight soaking time
COOK TIME: 45 minutes
PROCESSING TIME: 1 hour, 15 minutes
TOTAL TIME: 2 hours, 15 minutes, plus overnight soaking time

2¼ cups dried pinto beans
2½ pounds ground beef
1 cup chopped onion
¾ cup chopped peppers, bell, hot, or a combination
6 cups chopped tomatoes, fresh or canned
3 teaspoons chili powder
2 teaspoons salt
1 teaspoon freshly ground black pepper

DAY 1

In a large saucepot, combine the beans with enough water to cover. Soak for 12 hours, or overnight.

DAY 2

1. Drain the beans and return to the pot. Refill with fresh water. Bring to a boil. Reduce the heat to low and simmer for 30 minutes. Drain.

2. Prepare the jars, lids, and rings by washing them in hot, soapy water.

3. Place a rack in a pressure canner and add 3 to 4 inches of water. Fill the jars with a couple inches of water so they do not float, and place them in the canner. Bring the water to a simmer until ready to fill the jars. *Do not boil the water.*

4. In a large pot set over medium heat, combine the ground beef, onion, and peppers. Cook for about 10 minutes, or until the beef is browned and the onion softens. Add the beans, tomatoes, chili powder, salt, and pepper. Bring to a boil. Reduce the heat to low and simmer for 5 minutes.

5. Remove the jars from the canner, empty into the sink, and place them on a cutting board on a nearby countertop.

6. Ladle the chili into the prepared jars, leaving 1 inch of headspace. Use a nonmetallic utensil to release any air bubbles. Wipe the rims clean and seal with the lids and rings.

7. Put the jars on a rack in the pressure canner. Lock the lid in place, bring to a boil, and let the canner vent for 10 minutes. Put the weighted gauge or pressure regulator on the vent.

8. Process for 1 hour, 15 minutes at 11 pounds on a dial gauge or at 10 pounds on a weighted gauge. Adjust the pressure as necessary based on your altitude (see page 233). Adjust the temperature to maintain an even pressure. Turn off the heat. Let the pressure drop to zero before opening the lid.

9. Carefully remove the jars from the canner. Set aside to cool, undisturbed, for 12 hours.

10. Check the lids for proper seals (see page 32). Remove the rings, wipe the jars, label and date them, and transfer to a cupboard or pantry.

11. Refrigerate any jars that don't seal properly, and use within 3 days. Properly sealed jars will last in the cupboard for 12 months. Once opened, refrigerate and consume within 3 days.

VEGETARIAN CHILI

MAKES 5 PINT JARS

PRESSURE CANNING, LOW-SODIUM

Whether you eat meat or not, there is a place on your menu for vegetarian chili. This inexpensive blend is hearty and delicious, making it a perfect winter meal. Serve it topped with grated cheese and a piece of cornbread for a quick meal any night.

PREP TIME: 15 minutes, plus 1 hour soaking time
COOK TIME: 1 hour
PROCESSING TIME: 1 hour, 15 minutes
TOTAL TIME: 3 hours, 30 minutes

1 cup dried kidney beans
2 pounds tomatoes, skinned and chopped
1 cup chopped onion
3 garlic cloves, crushed
½ cup diced bell pepper, red, green, or yellow
1 jalapeño pepper, chopped
1 teaspoon ground cumin
2 teaspoons paprika
1 teaspoon dried oregano
1 teaspoon hot sauce

1. In a large saucepot set over high heat, combine the beans with enough water to cover. Bring to a boil. Cook for 2 minutes. Remove from heat and set aside, covered, for 1 hour.

2. Drain the beans and return them to the pot. Refill with fresh water. Bring to a boil. Reduce the heat to low and simmer for 30 minutes. Drain.

3. Prepare the jars, lids, and rings by washing them in hot, soapy water.

4. Place a rack in a pressure canner and add 3 to 4 inches of water. Fill the jars with a couple inches of water so they do not float, and place them in the canner. Bring the water to a simmer until ready to fill the jars. *Do not boil the water.*

5. In a large pot over medium-high heat, stir together the tomatoes, onion, garlic, bell pepper, jalapeño, cumin, paprika, oregano, and hot sauce. Bring to a boil. Reduce the heat to low. Simmer for 15 minutes. Add the beans and simmer for 10 minutes more.

6. Remove the jars from the canner, empty into the sink, and place them on a cutting board on a nearby countertop.

7. Ladle the chili into the prepared jars, leaving ½ inch of headspace. Use a nonmetallic utensil to release any air bubbles. Wipe the rims clean and seal with the lids and rings.

8. Put the jars on a rack in the pressure canner. Lock the lid in place, bring to a boil, and let the canner vent for 10 minutes. Put the weighted gauge or pressure regulator on the vent.

9. Process for 1 hour, 15 minutes at 11 pounds on a dial gauge or at 10 pounds on a weighted gauge. Adjust the pressure as necessary based on your altitude (see page 233). Adjust the temperature to maintain an even pressure. Turn off the heat. Let the pressure drop to zero before opening the lid.

10. Carefully remove the jars from the canner. Set aside to cool, undisturbed, for 12 hours.

11. Check the lids for proper seals (see page 32). Remove the rings, wipe the jars, label and date them, and transfer to a cupboard or pantry.

12. Refrigerate any jars that don't seal properly, and use within 3 days. Properly sealed jars will last in the cupboard for 12 months. Once opened, refrigerate and consume within 3 days.

BAKED BEANS

MAKES 7 PINT JARS

PRESSURE CANNING

Baked beans are an easy side dish that suits any meal—from extravagant to a campfire. When you make your own, you can control the amount of sugar and salt and create a tasty, traditionally seasoned product that tastes even better than store bought.

PREP TIME: 10 minutes
COOK TIME: 1 hour, 10 minutes, plus 1 hour soaking time
PROCESSING TIME: 1 hour, 5 minutes
TOTAL TIME: 3 hours, 25 minutes

8 cups dried navy beans
2 cups diced ham
8 cups tomato juice
1 cup firmly packed brown sugar
½ cup molasses
2 tablespoons salt
1 tablespoon white vinegar
1½ teaspoons ground mustard
½ teaspoon freshly ground black pepper

1. In a large pot set over medium-high heat, combine the beans with enough water to cover. Bring to a boil. Remove from the heat and set aside, covered, for 1 hour. Drain.

2. Prepare the jars, lids, and rings by washing them in hot, soapy water.

3. Place a rack in a pressure canner and add 3 to 4 inches of water. Fill the jars with a couple inches of water so they do not float, and place them in the canner. Bring the water to a simmer until ready to fill the jars. *Do not boil the water.*

4. Return the beans to the pot. Refill with enough fresh water to cover. Bring to a boil. Reduce the heat to low and simmer for about 1 hour, or until the beans are nearly done. Drain, return to the pot, cover, and keep warm.

5. In another large pot over medium-high heat, combine the ham, tomato juice, brown sugar, molasses, salt, white vinegar, ground mustard, and pepper. Bring to a boil. Reduce the heat to low. Simmer for 3 minutes. Add the beans. Stir to combine and heat through.

6. Remove the jars from the canner, empty into the sink, and place them on a cutting board on a nearby countertop.

7. Ladle the beans into the prepared jars, leaving 1 inch of headspace. Use a nonmetallic utensil to release any air bubbles. Wipe the rims clean and seal with the lids and rings.

8. Put the jars on a rack in the pressure canner. Lock the lid in place, bring to a boil, and let the canner vent for 10 minutes. Put the weighted gauge or pressure regulator on the vent.

9. Process for 1 hour, 5 minutes at 11 pounds on a dial gauge or at 10 pounds on a weighted gauge. Adjust the pressure as necessary based on your altitude (see page 233). Adjust the temperature to maintain an even pressure. Turn off the heat. Let the pressure drop to zero before opening the lid.

10. Carefully remove the jars from the canner. Set aside to cool, undisturbed, for 12 hours.

11. Check the lids for proper seals (see page 32). Remove the rings, wipe the jars, label and date them, and transfer to a cupboard or pantry.

12. Refrigerate any jars that don't seal properly, and use within 3 days. Properly sealed jars will last in the cupboard for 12 months. Once opened, refrigerate and consume within 3 days.

GROUND BEEF, LAMB, OR VENISON

MAKES 8 PINT JARS

PRESSURE CANNING

Canning meat may seem like a waste of time, but when you have pre-cooked meat ready to go in a dish on a busy night, it definitely takes on value. Look for meat on sale and stock up on this great all-purpose protein. You can shape the ground meat into meatballs or patties as long as they fit in the jars.

PREP TIME: 5 minutes
COOK TIME: 15 minutes
PROCESSING TIME: 1 hour, 15 minutes
TOTAL TIME: 1 hour, 35 minutes

8 pounds ground beef, lamb, or venison
4 teaspoons salt, divided
White vinegar, for cleaning the jars

1. Prepare the jars, lids, and rings by washing them in hot, soapy water.

2. Place a rack in a pressure canner and add 3 to 4 inches of water. Fill the jars with a couple inches of water so they do not float, and place them in the canner. Bring the water to a simmer until ready to fill the jars. *Do not boil the water.*

3. Fill a large pot with water and bring to a boil.

4. In a large skillet set over medium-high heat, cook the meat for about 10 minutes, or until lightly browned. Drain off any fat.

5. Working with one jar at a time, remove it from the canner, empty into the sink, and place on a cutting board on a nearby countertop.

6. Pack the meat into the prepared jar, leaving 1 inch of headspace. Add ½ teaspoon of salt per pint. Ladle in the boiling water, leaving 1 inch of headspace. Use a nonmetallic utensil to release any air bubbles. Wipe the rim of the jar with a solution of diluted vinegar and water to remove any greasy film. Seal with the lid and ring. Repeat with the remaining jars, meat, and salt.

7. Put the jars on a rack in the pressure canner. Lock the lid in place, bring to a boil, and let the canner vent for 10 minutes. Place a weighted gauge or pressure regulator on the vent.

8. Process for 1 hour, 15 minutes at 11 pounds on a dial gauge or at 10 pounds on a weighted gauge. Adjust the pressure as necessary based on your altitude (see page 233). Adjust the temperature to maintain an even pressure. Turn off the heat. Let the pressure drop to zero before opening the lid.

9. Carefully remove the jars from the canner. Set aside to cool, undisturbed, for 12 hours.

10. Check the lids for proper seals (see page 32). Remove the rings, wipe the jars, label and date them, and transfer to a cupboard or pantry.

11. Refrigerate any jars that don't seal properly, and use within 3 days. Properly sealed jars will last in the cupboard for 12 months. Once opened, refrigerate and consume within 3 days.

LOW-SODIUM PREPARATION TIP

The salt in this recipe is for flavor, not preservation. If you will be using the meat to prepare other dishes, consider omitting it and, instead, season the finished dish. This will cut down on sodium levels, while still ensuring a safe and flavorful canned meat.

TRY INSTEAD

Sausage can also be canned in the same way as other ground meats. However, one thing to avoid is seasoning the sausage with sage before canning, as it can produce a bitter flavor. If you are canning sausages in casings, remove the meat from the casing before browning and processing.

TRADITIONAL MINCEMEAT

MAKES 2 QUART JARS PLUS 2 PINT JARS

PRESSURE CANNING

The combination of spices and dried fruits produces a heady, intoxicating aroma—without any liquor. Use in a mincemeat pie, or simply spoon it onto crackers for a filling meal. If you'd rather try a mincemeat that doesn't have any meat in it, try Mock Mincemeat (see page 179).

PREP TIME: 15 minutes
COOK TIME: 2 hours
PROCESSING TIME: 1 hour, 30 minutes
TOTAL TIME: 3 hours, 45 minutes

½ cup finely chopped suet or beef fat
2 pounds ground beef, or venison
2½ quarts chopped apples
1 pound dark seedless raisins
1 pound golden raisins
5 cups sugar
1 quart apple cider
2 tablespoons salt
2 tablespoons ground cinnamon
2 teaspoons ground nutmeg

1. Prepare the jars, lids, and rings by washing them in hot, soapy water.

2. Place a rack in a pressure canner and add 3 to 4 inches of water. Fill the jars with a couple inches of water so they do not float, and place them in the canner. Bring the water to a simmer until ready to fill the jars. *Do not boil the water.*

3. In a large skillet or saucepan set over low heat, combine the suet, ground beef, and enough water to barely cover. Simmer for 15 to 20 minutes, or until the beef is completely cooked.

4. With a meat grinder or a food processor, grind together the cooked meat mixture, apples, dark raisins, and golden raisins. Transfer to a large saucepan set over low heat.

5. Add the sugar, apple cider, salt, cinnamon, and nutmeg. Simmer for 1 to 1½ hours, stirring frequently, or until very thick.

6. Remove the jars from the canner, empty into the sink, and place them on a cutting board on a nearby countertop.

7. Ladle the mincemeat into the prepared jars, leaving 1 inch of headspace. Use a nonmetallic utensil to release any air bubbles. Wipe the rims clean and seal with the lids and rings.

8. Put the jars on a rack in the pressure canner. Lock the lid in place, bring to a boil, and let the canner vent for 10 minutes. Put the weighted gauge or pressure regulator on the vent.

9. Process for 1 hour, 30 minutes at 11 pounds on a dial gauge or at 10 pounds on a weighted gauge. Adjust the pressure as necessary based on your altitude (see page 233). Adjust the temperature to maintain an even pressure. Turn off the heat. Let the pressure drop to zero before opening the lid.

10. Carefully remove the jars from the canner. Set aside to cool, undisturbed, for 12 hours.

11. Check the lids for proper seals (see page 32). Remove the rings, wipe the jars, label and date them, and transfer to a cupboard or pantry.

12. Refrigerate any jars that don't seal properly, and use within 5 days. Properly sealed jars will last in the cupboard for 12 months. Once opened, refrigerate and consume within 5 days.

SALMON

MAKES 4 PINT JARS

PRESSURE CANNING, SEASONAL

The key to canning fresh salmon is that the fish is cleaned promptly after catching. There is no need to debone the fish, as the bones will soften and provide beneficial calcium. Keep the salmon chilled until ready to can, at which time you will need to soak it in a salt-water brine. You can choose whether to keep or remove the skin. *Do not add any cooking liquid to the jars.* Wide-mouth jars are preferred for their ease of use when canning salmon.

PREP TIME: 5 minutes, plus 1 hour brining time
COOK TIME: 0
PROCESSING TIME: 1 hour, 40 minutes
TOTAL TIME: 2 hours, 45 minutes

1 cup pickling salt
1 gallon water
4 pounds salmon

1. In a large bowl, mix together the pickling salt and water until the salt is dissolved.

2. Cut the salmon into pieces that will fit into your jars. Submerge them in the brine and refrigerate for 1 hour. Weight with a clean plate, if necessary.

3. Prepare the jars, lids, and rings by washing them in hot, soapy water.

4. Place a rack in a pressure canner and add 3 to 4 inches of water.

5. In a colander over the sink, drain the salmon for 15 minutes.

6. Pack the salmon into **room-temperature jars**, skin-side facing the glass (if leaving on), leaving 1 inch of headspace. Use a nonmetallic utensil to release any air pockets. Wipe the rims clean, and seal with the lids and rings.

7. Put the jars on a rack in the pressure canner. Lock the lid in place, bring to a boil, and let the canner vent for 10 minutes. Put the weighted gauge or pressure regulator on the vent.

8. Process for 1 hour, 40 minutes at 11 pounds on a dial gauge or at 10 pounds on a weighted gauge. Adjust the pressure as necessary based on your altitude (see page 233). Adjust the temperature to maintain an even pressure. Turn off the heat. Let the pressure drop to zero before opening the lid.

9. Carefully remove the jars from the canner. Set aside to cool, undisturbed, for 12 hours.

10. Check the lids for proper seals (see page 32). Remove the rings, wipe the jars, label and date them, and transfer to a cupboard or pantry.

11. Refrigerate any jars that don't seal properly, and use within 3 days. Properly sealed jars will last in the cupboard for 12 months. Once opened, refrigerate and consume within 3 days.

PREPARATION TIP

When pressure canning oily foods such as meats and fish, it is helpful to add a couple tablespoons of vinegar to the water in the canner. This makes cleanup quicker by making it easier to wash away any grease that accumulates on the jars or canner.

TUNA

MAKES 12 TO 13 HALF-PINT JARS

PRESSURE CANNING, SEASONAL, LOW-SODIUM

Plan for about one hour to prep and pack the tuna. Take extra care to separate the dark flesh from the white flesh so the end product tastes best. Canning only the white flesh allows you to can the tuna from its raw state, which is simplest. Like other fish, skin it, remove the viscera, bleed, and debone the fish promptly after catching. Use wide-mouth jars when possible to make packing easier, and screw the rings on the jars while packing to prevent a ton of greasy buildup on the mouths of the jars.

PREP TIME: 1 hour
COOK TIME: 0
PROCESSING TIME: 1 hour, 40 minutes
TOTAL TIME: 2 hours, 40 minutes

15 pounds tuna steaks, white flesh separated for canning
White vinegar, for cleaning the jars

1. Prepare the jars, lids, and rings by washing them in hot, soapy water.

2. Place a rack in a pressure canner and add 3 to 4 inches of water.

3. Pack the tuna into **room-temperature jars**, leaving a generous 1-inch headspace. If possible, place whole chunks of tuna steaks into each jar and then pack full with smaller pieces. Use a nonmetallic utensil to release any air pockets. With a kitchen towel soaked in white vinegar, wipe the rims and sides of each jar to remove any oil or small bits of tuna. Seal with the lids and rings.

4. Put the jars on the rack in the pressure canner. Lock the lid in place, bring to a boil, and let the canner vent for 10 minutes. Put the weighted gauge or pressure regulator on the vent.

5. Process for 1 hour, 40 minutes at 11 pounds on a dial gauge or at 10 pounds on a weighted gauge. Adjust the pressure as necessary based on your altitude (see page 233). Adjust the temperature to maintain an even pressure. Turn off the heat. Let the pressure drop to zero before opening the lid.

6. Carefully remove the jars from the canner. Set aside to cool, undisturbed, for 12 hours.

7. Check the lids for proper seals (see page 32). Remove the rings, wipe the jars with a vinegar-soaked cloth, label and date them, and transfer to a cupboard or pantry.

8. Refrigerate any jars that don't seal properly, and use within 3 days. Properly sealed jars will last in the cupboard for 12 months. Once opened, refrigerate and consume within 3 days.

CLOSER LOOK

Tuna is a highly seasonal product, typically most widely available from late June or early July through September, depending on your location. For best results, buy tuna directly off fishing boats, or from a reliable and trusted fishmonger. Because of the strong smell tuna can impart to your kitchen, this is a great time to put to work a camp stove or outdoor cooktop you might have, and do some outdoor canning.

APPENDIX A

ALTITUDE ADJUSTMENTS

To make safe adjustments for canning at altitudes greater than 1,000 feet, use the following guidelines and consult resources such as the USDA's *Complete Guide to Home Canning* for more information. To find out your exact altitude, you can contact your local county extension agent or the local district conservationist for the Soil Conservation Service.

The technique for safe canning (see page 15) is the same, no matter what your altitude.

For **water-bath canning**, increase processing time as noted below based on your altitude.

ALTITUDE IN FEET	INCREASE PROCESSING TIME
0 to 1,000	no adjustment needed
1,001 to 3,000	5 minutes
3,001 to 6,000	10 minutes
6,001 to 8,000	15 minutes
8,001 to 10,000	20 minutes

For **pressure canning**, adjust pressure as noted below based on your altitude.

ALTITUDE IN FEET	DIAL GAUGE CANNER	WEIGHTED GAUGE CANNER
0 to 1,000	11	10
1,001 to 2,000	11	15
2,001 to 4,000	12	15
4,001 to 6,000	13	15
6,001 to 8,000	14	15
8,001 to 10,000	15	15

APPENDIX B

PH RANGES OF COMMON FOODS

The pH scale ranges from 0 to 14, and measures how acidic or alkaline a food is. The lower the pH value, the more acidic the food. The general rule of thumb is that high-acid foods (with a pH less than 4.6) are generally safe for hot water-bath canning. Foods with a pH of 4.7 or higher are low acid. These foods must be processed in a pressure canner or can be pickled to make them safe for hot water processing.

This list is based on the latest information available from the FDA/Center for Food Safety and Applied Nutrition. You can find methods and conditions for determining the pH and acidity of foods summarized in the document titled 21 CFR 114.90, available online or from the Government Printing Office.

ITEM	APPROXIMATE PH
Anchovies	6.50
Anchovies, stuffed with capers, in olive oil	5.58
Apples, Delicious	3.90
Apples, Golden Delicious	3.60
Apples, Jonathan	3.33
Apples, McIntosh	3.34
Apples, Winesap	3.47
Apricots	3.30 to 4.80
Artichokes	5.50 to 6.00
Avocados	6.27 to 6.58
Baby corn	5.20
Bamboo shoots	5.10 to 6.20
Bananas	4.50 to 5.20
Beans	5.60 to 6.50
Black	5.78 to 6.02
Boston baked	5.05 to 5.42
Kidney	5.40 to 6.00
Lima	6.50
Soy	6.00 to 6.60
String	5.60
Wax	5.30 to 5.70
Beets	5.30 to 6.60
Blackberries	3.85 to 4.50
Blueberries	3.12 to 3.33
Broccoli	6.30 to 6.85
Brussels sprouts	6.00 to 6.30
Buttermilk	4.41 to 4.83
Cabbage, green	5.50 to 6.75

ITEM	APPROXIMATE PH
Cabbage, red	5.60 to 6.00
Cabbage, savoy	6.30
Cabbage, white	6.20
Cactus	4.70
Calamari (squid)	5.80
Cantaloupe	6.13 to 6.58
Capers	6.00
Carrots	5.88 to 6.40
Cauliflower	5.60
Caviar, American	5.70 to 6.00
Celery	5.70 to 6.00
Chayote, cooked	6.00 to 6.30
Cherries	4.01 to 4.54
Chicory	5.90 to 6.05
Chives	5.20 to 6.31
Clams	6.00 to 7.10
Coconut, fresh	5.50 to 7.80
Corn	5.90 to 7.30
Crab meat	6.50 to 7.00
Cream, 20 percent	6.50 to 6.68
Cucumbers	5.12 to 5.78
Dates	4.14 to 4.88
Eel	6.20
Eggplant	5.50 to 6.50
Eggs, whites	7.96
Eggs, whole	6.58
Eggs, yolks	6.10
Escarole	5.70 to 6.00
Fennel	5.48 to 5.88
Figs, Calimyrna	5.05 to 5.98
Garlic	5.80
Ginger	5.60 to 5.90
Gooseberries	2.80 to 3.10
Grapefruit	3.00 to 3.75
Grapes, Concord	2.80 to 3.00
Hearts of palm	5.70
Herring	6.10
Honey	3.70 to 4.20

ITEM	APPROXIMATE PH
Horseradish, freshly grated	5.35
Jackfruit	4.80 to 6.80
Kelp	6.30
Kumquat	3.64 to 4.25
Leeks	5.50 to 6.17
Lemon juice	2.00 to 2.60
Lime	2.00 to 2.80
Loganberries	2.70 to 3.50
Loquat	5.10
Lotus root	6.90
Lychee	4.70 to 5.01
Mangos, green	5.80 to 6.00
Mangos, ripe	3.40 to 4.80
Maple syrup	5.15
Mayhaw (a variety of strawberry)	3.27 to 3.86
Melon, casaba	5.78 to 6.00
Melon, honeydew	6.00 to 6.67
Melon, Persian	5.90 to 6.38
Milk, cow	6.40 to 6.80
Milk, goat	6.48
Milk, soybean	7.00
Molasses	4.90 to 5.40
Mushrooms	6.00 to 6.70
Mussels	6.00 to 6.85
Mustard	3.55 to 6.00
Nectarines	3.92 to 4.18
Octopus	6.00 to 6.50
Onions, red	5.30 to 5.80
Onions, white	5.37 to 5.85
Onions, yellow	5.32 to 5.60
Oranges	3.69 to 4.34
Oysters	5.68 to 6.17
Oysters, smoked	6.00
Oyster mushrooms	5.00 to 6.00
Papaya	5.20 to 6.00
Parsley	5.70 to 6.00
Parsnip	5.30 to 5.70
Peaches	3.30 to 4.05

ITEM	APPROXIMATE PH
Pears, Bartlett	3.50 to 4.60
Peppers, green	5.20 to 5.93
Persimmons	4.42 to 4.70
Pineapple	3.20 to 4.00
Plums, blue	2.80 to 3.40
Plums, damson	2.90 to 3.10
Plums, red	3.60 to 4.30
Plums, yellow	3.90 to 4.45
Pomegranate	2.93 to 3.20
Potatoes	5.40 to 5.90
Pumpkin	4.90 to 5.50
Quince	3.12 to 3.40
Radishes, red	5.85 to 6.05
Radishes, white	5.52 to 5.69
Raisins, seedless	3.80 to 4.10
Raspberries	3.22 to 3.95
Rhubarb	3.10 to 3.40
Romaine	5.78 to 6.06
Salmon, fresh, broiled	5.36 to 6.40
Sardines	5.70 to 6.60
Scallion	6.20
Scallop	6.00
Sherry wine	3.37
Shrimp	6.50 to 7.00

ITEM	APPROXIMATE PH
Spinach	5.50 to 6.80
Squid	6.00 to 6.50
Strawberries	3.00 to 3.90
Straw mushroom	4.90
Sturgeon	6.20
Sweet potatoes	5.30 to 5.60
Tamarind	3.00
Tangerine	3.32 to 4.48
Tea	7.20
Tofu	7.20
Tomatillo	3.83
Tomatoes	4.30 to 4.90
Tomatoes, canned	3.50 to 4.70
Tomatoes, vine ripened	4.42 to 4.65
Truffles	5.30 to 6.50
Tuna fish, canned	5.90 to 6.20
Turnips	5.29 to 5.90
Vegetable juice	3.90 to 4.30
Vinegar, cider	3.10
Walnuts, English	5.42
Water chestnut	6.00 to 6.20
Watercress	5.88 to 6.18
Watermelon	5.18 to 5.60
Worcestershire sauce	3.63 to 4.00

APPENDIX C

THE DIRTY DOZEN & THE CLEAN FIFTEEN

A nonprofit and environmental watchdog organization called Environmental Working Group (EWG) looks at data supplied by the US Department of Agriculture (USDA) and the Food and Drug Administration (FDA) about pesticide residues and compiles a list each year of the best and worst pesticide loads found in commercial crops. You can use these lists to decide which fruits and vegetables to buy organic to minimize your exposure to pesticides and which produce is considered safe enough to skip the organics. This does not mean they are pesticide-free, though, so wash these fruits and vegetables thoroughly.

These lists change every year, so make sure you look up the most recent before you fill your shopping cart. You'll find the most recent lists as well as a guide to pesticides in produce at EWG.org/FoodNews.

2015 DIRTY DOZEN

- Apples
- Celery
- Cherry tomatoes
- Cucumbers
- Grapes
- Nectarines
- Peaches
- Potatoes
- Snap peas (imported)
- Spinach
- Strawberries
- Sweet bell peppers

In addition to the dirty dozen, the EWG added two American food crops laced with particularly toxic pesticides:

- Kale/collard greens
- Hot peppers

2015 CLEAN FIFTEEN

- Asparagus
- Avocados
- Cabbage
- Cantaloupes
- Cauliflower
- Eggplants
- Grapefruits
- Kiwis
- Mangoes
- Onions
- Papayas
- Pineapples
- Sweet corn
- Sweet peas (frozen)
- Sweet potatoes

APPENDIX D

MEASUREMENT CONVERSIONS

VOLUME EQUIVALENTS (LIQUID)

US STANDARD	US STANDARD (OUNCES)	METRIC (APPROXIMATE)
2 tablespoons	1 fl. oz.	30 mL
¼ cup	2 fl. oz.	60 mL
½ cup	4 fl. oz.	120 mL
1 cup	8 fl. oz.	240 mL
1½ cups	12 fl. oz.	355 mL
2 cups or 1 pint	16 fl. oz.	475 mL
4 cups or 1 quart	32 fl. oz.	1 L
1 gallon	128 fl. oz.	4 L

OVEN TEMPERATURES

FAHRENHEIT (F)	CELSIUS (C) (APPROXIMATE)
250°	120°
300°	150°
325°	165°
350°	180°
375°	190°
400°	200°
425°	220°
450°	230°

VOLUME EQUIVALENTS (DRY)

US STANDARD	METRIC (APPROXIMATE)
⅛ teaspoon	0.5 mL
¼ teaspoon	1 mL
½ teaspoon	2 mL
¾ teaspoon	4 mL
1 teaspoon	5 mL
1 tablespoon	15 mL
¼ cup	59 mL
⅓ cup	79 mL
½ cup	118 mL
⅔ cup	156 mL
¾ cup	177 mL
1 cup	235 mL
2 cups or 1 pint	475 mL
3 cups	700 mL
4 cups or 1 quart	1 L

WEIGHT EQUIVALENTS

US STANDARD	METRIC (APPROXIMATE)
½ ounce	15 g
1 ounce	30 g
2 ounces	60 g
4 ounces	115 g
8 ounces	225 g
12 ounces	340 g
16 ounces or 1 pound	455 g

GLOSSARY

ACETIC ACID. The component of vinegar that gives it a soured taste. The clear, liquid acid is the primary acid in vinegar. For pickling, vinegar must have 5 percent acetic acid.

ASCORBIC ACID. Another name for vitamin C. A water-soluble vitamin that is used in food preparation to minimize browning of some vegetables and fruits. Often used together with citric acid, which is derived from lemon or lime juice, in commercially prepared blends to treat fruits to prevent browning.

BACTERIA. Microorganisms found in the air, soil, and water. Harmful bacteria can survive in low-acid environments and produce toxins that can be deadly. For this reason, low-acid foods are pressure canned to enable heating to 240°F, a temperature that kills these bacteria.

BLANCH. The process of placing a food item in boiling water or steam for a short period of time. Blanching is always followed by an ice water bath to quickly cool the food item and prevent further cooking. This process is used to inactivate enzymes in foods, as well as to loosen the skin or peel of some fruits and vegetables.

BOIL. Bringing a liquid to the temperature in which bubbles continuously break its surface. At sea level, the boiling point is 212°F, while at altitudes above 1,000 feet, this is achieved at a lower temperature.

BOIL, FULL ROLLING. Boiling that cannot be stirred down. This type of boiling, often accompanied by foaming, is essential when making cooked jams and jellies. The temperature to achieve a rolling boil is 220°F.

BOTULISM. A deadly form of food poisoning caused by the bacterium *Clostridium botulinum*. These spores are present in the soil and air around us, but are able to activate only when there is a lack of oxygen and low acid levels. For this reason, it is highly important to process low-acid foods properly, for the recommended length and temperature, to kill the spores that produce this toxin.

BRINE. A solution used in the pickling process. Typically contains salt and water, although other ingredients such as spices or sugar can also be included.

BUTTER (FRUIT). A soft spread created using puréed fruit and sugar cooked over a low temperature until thickened. Best for tree fruits (apples, apricots, nectarines, peaches, pears, plums) and tropical fruits (guava, mango, passion fruit, pineapple).

CANDY THERMOMETER. A type of cooking thermometer that is fitted with clips or hooks to attach it to a pan. Used primarily in jam and jelly making to determine when the product will gel, which is typically around 220°F.

CANNING LIQUID. Any liquid used in canning to cover food products in the jar. This can be water, brine, broth, syrup, or juice. The liquid is instrumental to heat penetration in the jar, as well as preventing foods from darkening.

CHEESE. A sliceable preserve, typically made from tree fruits (apples, apricots, nectarines, peaches, pears, plums) and tropical fruits (guava, mango, passion fruit, pineapple).

CHEESECLOTH. A woven cloth designed for kitchen use. Used to drain juice from fruits and to form a spice bag to hold whole spices during cooking.

CHUTNEY. A sweet and sour condiment made from fruits or vegetables, vinegar, and spices. Best when cured for at least one month after canning to ensure flavors are well blended.

CITRIC ACID. An acid derived from citrus fruit. It is found in pectin and assists with gel formation, as well as commercial produce protectors to prevent oxidation of light-colored fruits.

CLEARJEL. A thickening agent made from modified food starch that does not break down when heated to high temperatures or reheated after cooling. Commercially available and approved by the USDA for use in home canning.

CONSERVE. Made from a combination of fruits, often including nuts, and frequently served with roasted meats. Best for citrus fruits, berries (blackberries, blueberries, currants, raspberries, strawberries), tree fruits (apples, apricots, nectarines, peaches, pears, plums), tropical fruits (guava, mango, passion fruit, pineapple), grapes, and peppers (bell peppers, chiles).

CURD. A thick spread typically made from citrus fruit (lemon, lime, tangerine, orange). Curds have more juice and zest than other spreads, giving them an intense fruit flavor that pairs well with cakes, tarts, breads, and scones.

ENZYME. A protein found in foods that begins the process of decomposition. Enzymes can change the texture, color, and flavor of fruits and vegetables. Food preservation methods deactivate these enzymes to permit long-term storage of foods.

FOOD MILL. A mechanical kitchen tool used to purée soft foods. A food mill separates the skins and seeds of the fruits or vegetables on its top, and the puréed food is collected below.

FRESH-PACK PICKLES. Pickles created by canning cucumbers in a brine solution without fermentation. In some cases, these cucumbers are brined before canning. For the best flavor, fresh-pack pickles should be left to sit for 4 to 6 weeks before eating.

HEADSPACE. The space at the top of a canning jar that is left unfilled. Headspace varies based on the food type and is essential for creating a proper seal.

HOT-PACK METHOD. Using preheated, hot food to fill jars prior to processing them in a hot water bath. Filling jars with preheated food expels air and allows food to be packed more tightly.

JAM. A soft, thick spreadable preserve containing one or more crushed fruits and sugar. Commercial pectin is optional. Best for berries (blackberries, blueberries, currants, raspberries, strawberries), tree fruits (apples, apricots, nectarines, peaches, pears, plums), tropical fruits (guava, mango, passion fruit, pineapple), grapes, and peppers (bell peppers, chiles).

JELLY. A clear, spreadable, soft preserve made with fruit juice and sugar. Commercial pectin is optional. Best for berries (blackberries, blueberries, currants, raspberries, strawberries), tree fruits (apples, apricots, nectarines, peaches, pears, plums), tropical fruits (guava, mango, passion fruit, pineapple), grapes, and peppers (bell peppers, chiles).

LEMON JUICE. The juice extracted from lemons. In jam making, lemon juice is used to assist with the gelling of the finished product. In most other home canning recipes, it is used to ensure the proper acid of the finished product. Because the acid in fresh lemons is variable, it is important to use bottled lemon juice when the recipe specifies it to ensure the safety of the finished product. When fresh lemon juice is called for, either bottled or fresh can be used.

MARMALADE. Made from the peel and juice of citrus fruits macerated then cooked in sugar. Known for its bitter flavor. Best for citrus fruits (grapefruits, lemons, limes, Seville or sour oranges) and ginger.

PRESERVE. A soft spread made with fruit and sugar. Preserves often have whole fruit pieces in them and can vary considerably in thickness, but typically do not hold their shape when spooned from the jar.

PRESSURE CANNER. A tall pot with a locking lid, rack, and a pressure regulating mechanism. Used to process low-acid foods as pressure enables the jars to reach 240°F, the temperature needed to kill harmful bacteria.

RELISH. Pickled spread made from diced fruits and/or vegetables cooked in a vinegar solution. Can be flavored sweet with the addition of sugar, or spicy with the addition of hot peppers.

SACHET (OR SPICE BAG). A small bag (made from muslin), or cheesecloth square secured with kitchen twine, used to hold whole spices while cooking in liquid to infuse their flavor into the finished product.

SYRUP. Sweetened and lightly thickened juice from fruits and some vegetables. Best for berries (blackberries, blueberries, currants, raspberries, strawberries), citrus fruits, ginger, rhubarb, tree fruits (apples, apricots, nectarines, peaches, pears, plums), tropical fruits (guava, mango, passion fruit, pineapple), grapes, and peppers (bell peppers, chiles).

VENTING. The process used in pressure canning where the vent is left open while the water boils below. This allows for the air to escape the canner before fixing it with the pressure gauge.

VINEGAR, APPLE CIDER. A vinegar produced from apples that has a tart, fruity flavor. Cider vinegar has a golden color and may discolor some canned foods. Always use 5 percent acidity when using cider vinegar for canning.

VINEGAR, WHITE. A standard type of vinegar produced from grain alcohol. It is clear and colorless, making it suitable for a lot of different canning projects, as it does not compete with the colors or flavors of the foods. Always use 5 percent acidity vinegar when canning.

WATER-BATH CANNER. A large pot and lid fixed with a rack to keep jars lifted away from the direct heat. The pot must be deep enough so jars are covered by 1 inch of water, as well as to allow the water to boil rapidly.

WHOLE, OR CUT, FRUITS IN A SYRUP. Best for berries (blackberries, blueberries, currants, raspberries, strawberries), tree fruits (apples, apricots, nectarines, peaches, pears, plums), tropical fruits (guava, mango, passion fruit, pineapple), grapes, and peppers (bell peppers, chiles).

RESOURCES

GENERAL INFORMATION

Information, help, and resources for home food preservation.

Azam-Ali, Dr. Sue, and Mike Battcock. "Fermented Fruits and Vegetables: A Global Perspective." *Food and Agricultural Organization Services Bulletin*, no. 134, 1998.

Bord Biá, Irish Food Board. *Traditional Foods Skills for Tomorrow: Food Heritage in Living Memory*. Accessed February 7, 2015. www.bordbia.ie/consumer/aboutfood/Documents/Traditional%20Food%20skills%20-%20Food%20heritage%20in%20living%20memory.pdf.

Food and Agriculture Organization. *Manual on Simple Methods of Food Preservation*. Food and Agriculture Organization of the United Nations, 1990.

International Pectin Producers Association. "What Is Pectin?" *Facts About Pectin*. Accessed July 7, 2014. www.ippa.info/history_of_pectin.htm.

Katz, Sandor Ellix. *The Art of Fermentation: An In-Depth Exploration of Essential Concepts and Processes from Around the World*. White River Junction, VT: Chelsea Green Publishing, 2012.

Krissoff, Liana. *Canning for a New Generation*. New York City, NY: Stewart, Tabori & Chang, 2010.

Lampe, Johanna, W. "Fermented Foods: Intake and Implications for Cancer." AICR 2013 Annual Research Conference on Food, Nutrition, Physical Activity and Cancer. American Institute of Cancer Research. Accessed February 7, 2015. www.aicr.org/assets/docs/pdf/research/rescon2013/lampe-fermented-foods.pdf.

Lewin, Alex. *Real Food Fermentation: Preserving Whole Fresh Food with Live Cultures in Your Home Kitchen*. Minneapolis, MN: Quarry Books, 2012.

McClellan, Marisa. *Food in Jars*. Philadelphia, PA: Running Press Book Publishers, 2011.

Mother Earth News. "Home Canning Guide: Learn How to Can Your Own Food." Accessed July 5, 2014. www.motherearthnews.com/real-food/canning.aspx#axzz352y94KKH.

National Center for Home Food Preservation. "Preserving Food at Home." Accessed July 5, 2014. https://spock.fcs.uga.edu/ext/food/nchfp_elc/.

Penn State Extension. "Avoid…Open Kettle or Oven Canning." Accessed February 7, 2015. http://extension.psu.edu/food/preservation/news/2014/avoid-open-kettle-canning.

Penn State Extension. "Home Food Preservation News." Accessed July 5, 2014. http://extension.psu.edu/food/preservation.

Peterson, Sharon. "Pressure Canning: How to Can with a Pressure Canner." *Simply Canning*. Accessed July 5, 2014. www.simplycanning.com/pressure-canning.html.

Preserve. *All About Pectin for Jam, Jellies and Preserves*. www.portlandpreserve.com/all%20about%20pectin%20for%20jam%20makers.pdf.

Time-Life Books. *Preserving*. Morristown, NJ: Time-Life Books, 1981.

U.S. Food and Drug Administration. "Foodborne Illness and Contaminants." Accessed February 7, 2015. www.fda.gov/food/foodborneillnesscontaminants/default.htm.

Valigra, Lori. "The Father of Food Preservation." *Food Quality and Safety*. February/March 2011.

Varozza, Georgia. *The Amish Canning Cookbook*. Eugene, OR: Harvest House Publishers, 2013.

WSU/Whatcom County Cooperative Extension. *Crisp Pickles*. Accessed July 5, 2014. whatcom.wsu.edu/family/facts/crisppickles.htm.

Ziedrich, Linda. *The Joy of Jams, Jellies, and Other Sweet Preserves*. Boston, MA: The Harvard Common Press, 2009.

INGREDIENTS AND SUPPLIES

There are a few items that might be difficult to find at the usual spots. The following are resources that carry a range of ingredients for preserving—from special salt and alum to spices and herbs.

Canning Supply: A source for hard-to-find items like picking lime and alum. Accessed July 5, 2014. www.canningsupply.com/.

Pick Your Own. "Picking Tips for Fruits and Vegetables." Accessed July 5, 2014. www.pickyourown.org/pickingtips.htm.

Pomona's Universal Pectin. Accessed July 5, 2014. www.pomonapectin.com/.

EQUIPMENT

Traditional canning jars manufactured by Ball and Kerr are widely available in many stores, from grocery stores to home-goods stores and garden centers.

Ace Hardware. "Home Canning." Accessed July 5, 2014. www.acehardware.com/.

Williams Sonoma. "Canning and Preserving." Accessed July 5, 2014. www.williams-sonoma.com/shop/agrarian-garden/agrarian-canning-preserving/.

REFERENCES

Bush, Deidre, Katherine Clayton, and Kevin Keener. "Food Preservation Methods." West Lafayette, IN: Purdue University Department of Food and Science, March 14, 2012.

Gunders, Dana. "Wasted: How America Is Losing up to 40 Percent of Its Food from Farm to Fork to Landfill." New York City, NY: National Resources Defense Council, August 2012.

Henderson, Judy and Carrie Thompson. "Making Pickles in North Carolina." Raleigh, NC: North Carolina Cooperative Extension Service. Accessed July 5, 2014. fbns.ncsu.edu/extension_program/documents/foodsafety_making_pickles_in_NC.pdf.

National Center for Emerging and Zoonotic Infectious Diseases. "Botulism." Atlanta, GA: Centers for Disease Control and Prevention, last modified April 25, 2014. www.cdc.gov/nczved/divisions/dfbmd/diseases/botulism/.

National Center for Home Food Preservation. "Frequently Asked Canning Questions." Accessed on July 5, 2014. nchfp.uga.edu/questions/FAQ_canning.html#3.

National Nutrient Database. Beltsville, MD: USDA Agricultural Research Service, revised December 7, 2011.

Oehler, Nellie. "Low Sugar Jams and Jellies." Corvallis, OR: Oregon State University Extension Service, revised March 1998.

Oregon State University Extension Service. "Low Salt Pickles." Corvallis, OR: Oregon State University, revised February 2013.

West, Kevin. *Saving the Season: A Cook's Guide to Home Canning, Pickling, and Preserving*. New York City, NY: Knopf Doubleday Publishing Group, 2013.

PROCESSING TYPE INDEX

PRESSURE CANNING

WATER-BATH CANNING

INGREDIENTS INDEX

INDEX

Y

Z

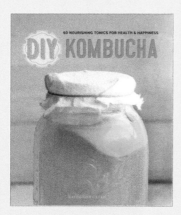

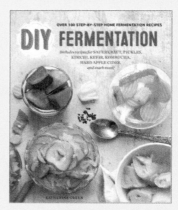

CPSIA information can be obtained at www.ICGtesting.com
Printed in the USA
BVOW10s1656050715

407137BV00002B/2/P